The Allotment Diaries

THE ALLOTMENT DIARIES

Summersdale Publishers Ltd
46 West Street
Chichester
West Sussex
PO19 1RP
UK

www.summersdale.com

Printed and bound by CPI Group (UK) Ltd, Croydon, CR0 4YY

ISBN: 978-1-84953-355-3

Substantial discounts on bulk quantities of Summersdale books are available to corporations, professional associations and other organisations. For details contact Nicky Douglas by telephone: +44 (0) 1243 756902, fax: +44 (0) 1243 786300 or email: nicky@summersdale.com.

The Allotment Diaries

A year of potting, plotting and feasting

Kay Sexton

summersdale

Acknowledgements

This book would not exist without 'The Committee' who keep our allotment site going and the council team who work tirelessly (and often thanklessly) to keep our city's allotments safe, available and affordable; the many veteran growers who have, over decades, shared their time, experience and advice with a generosity that is typical of the allotment community; Brie, who is the most green-fingered of agents; and the team at Summersdale who make it a pleasure to write about my passion. Above all, once again, I thank my parents and OH for giving me the love, support and encouragement to grow food and to write about the process.

Contents

AUTUMN

WINTER

Preamble

There's one big problem with calling a book 'The Allotment Diaries' – and that's the fact that any diary, based around allotment life, is going to seem completely implausible and unlikely to many of its readers. Not that they would object to the stories of remarkable folk I've met and their fascinating lives – those bits resonate with most allotment-holders and when I give readings from *Minding My Peas and Cucumbers*, my first book on the subject, there's always somebody in the audience who thinks I'm writing about their allotment site, or who has had a virtually identical experience with an allotment neighbour. No, it's the horticulture that people will think I'm making up!

Britain has one of the most variable meteorological systems in the world, along with complex geology. Those two factors combine to ensure that the conditions in which I grow food will probably be different to the conditions in which people reading this book grow food. Some of the differences may be subtle: a frost date that's a few weeks earlier (anybody north of Birmingham) or a few weeks later (anybody south-west of Southampton), or they may be gigantic: my struggles with clay soil will not make much sense to Fenlanders with their blessed rich and friable loam and folk with vegetable gardens in County Down will laugh derisively at what I call a gale – they call it a breeze!

So you may be wondering what use this book will be to you. It's a fair question. The answer is that good growing, like most things, takes practice and experience and all information is simply indicative of how to begin that practice and how to develop some personal experience. I teach allotment skills on my plot and every year somebody will mutter disgustedly that you can't trust seed packets because the instructions don't work. It's true they don't, a lot of the time, and that's because any 'average' information written to cover the range of potential soils, weather and knowledge in the British population will inevitably fail to meet the requirements of the soil, climate and knowledge at each of the extreme ends of 'average'. My friend Celia can look at a seed and with one piece of information – the geographic location to which it is native – work out the necessary growing conditions, but her knowledge is encyclopaedic and she has a lifetime of experience. I need a lot more information than that, but I am pretty good at adapting general information to the specific circumstances of my plot, my soil, my time constraints, my willingness to cater to fussy plants, etc. Learning is based on earning, and you earn knowledge through the cycles of the allotment year and through being alert to what works and what doesn't – for you.

Each of us can become proficient at growing vegetables, flowers and fruit, and a large part of proficiency is based on experience that comes from adjusting general information like 'plant potatoes at Easter' to local conditions. Find out your first and last frost dates, if you haven't kept track of them in the past, and base *your* sowing, planting out and harvesting on them, not on calendar dates. Watch what more experienced growers do, but don't listen to what they say (they lie, like fishermen, to impress) and if you must listen, before you take their words as gospel, get a look at their harvest.

In my early years of allotment life I was a credulous simpleton who believed whatever any man wearing a flat cap and braces told me. It wasn't until I learned to look at the food they produced that I realised they weren't necessarily experts and often did things *they* had been told to do without ever testing the advice to see if it produced good results. As an example, people used to trim leek roots before planting them out, until several reliable field trials proved that this actually harmed growth – but when I first started allotment growing old guard members told me my leeks would come to nothing if I didn't cut back the roots. They were wrong, scientifically proven to be wrong, but I don't think pointing this out to them ever changed their minds or their methods – or improved the size of their leeks!

Good growers are flexible, they keep reasonable records and they try new things with a sceptical but willing attitude. Approach this book in the same way. If I make a suggestion that clearly wouldn't work for your growing conditions, it doesn't mean the rest of the book won't be useful, it just means our situations with regard to that crop, or that month, are not identical. If something does seem plausible, give it a test – you don't have to change the habits of a lifetime overnight but you can, for example, plant half your leeks with trimmed roots and half with untrimmed and compare the results when you harvest them. And let me know what works for you!

SPRING

March

3 March

I have been invited to visit Celia, my clever, polyglot, plant-conserving friend. There are two ways that I interact with Celia – my favourite is the casual way we bump into each other around the allotments, or just happen to be in the same place at the same time, usually at a plant sale or a seed swap or some other horticultural happening.

The other way is the one I don't like nearly as much: it's when I get a summons by telephone to Celia and Stefan's house and it's usually the prelude to an announcement. Sometimes the summons isn't clear – I pick up my mobile, see that Celia has called, and then listen to a message that sounds like a Dalek reading Klingon through a tannoy. The first time this happened I was perturbed, but after years of experience I have learned to accept that Celia has just remembered she wants to talk to me, and that her intellect is translating one complex language (say Latvian) to another (perhaps Macedonian) at the same time her hands are reshaping a hundred-year-old bonsai tree with her phone set to hands-free. So at the instant that the thought strikes, she leaves me a message in whatever language is uppermost in her mind, the end result of which is a tinny incomprehensible string of consonants on my phone.

When I arrive she is reading *The Waste Land* aloud to one of her cats. This is not an unusual scenario in Celia's house in March and I slide into a chair and wait for her to finish. She closes the book and turns to me with the martyred expression of a woman in torment yet determined to be stoical. She's good at martyred stoicism; her slim, chiselled blondeness and energetic air often suggest to me what Joan of Arc might have grown up to look like if she'd escaped the flames.

'I have lost all my *Tillandsias*,' she says in muted tones. I nod sombrely and make a mental note to look up *Tillandsia* when I get home.

She hands me a propagator in which are two small pots. In each pot a single seedling of extremely unprepossessing appearance lolls like a consumptive orphan in a Dickens novel.

'It could be an airborne bacterium – we're disinfecting everything!'

I look at the cat, who appears long-suffering and clean; when Celia does things, she does them thoroughly.

She continues, 'In the meantime, other potentially susceptible plants have to be removed from the danger zone. You are an isolation ward. Guard these with your life,' she finishes, rather dramatically.

I make another mental note that if I can't keep these two plants alive I had better arrange to meet Celia in a place free from blades and blunt weapons to announce my failure, and drive home with the propagator nestled into the seatbelt beside me and a sheaf of notes on the seedlings' daily care tucked into my bag.

This is a regular spring operation for those of us who know Celia – she propagates and germinates a vast range of almost impossible to grow plants, but March is the cruellest month and she has learned to distribute her tender young seedlings amongst her friends so that if damp, blight, cat romping or Acts of God destroy what she has raised, she may still have a few seedlings boarded out amongst her acquaintance. Having just lost all her *Tillandsias* (whatever they may be) to Persephone (Celia is a classicist) she has been driven to desperation, as a result of which I am entrusted with two of some other variety of precious seedling in case the goddess hasn't quite finished with Celia yet.

17 March

My new infants are being nurtured as I have been instructed. They aren't exactly thriving but they are still alive. Daily I turn their pots, check their temperature and humidity and do everything short of reading aloud to them. They still look Dickensian but are now more like members of Fagin's gang than Little Nell: they are ugly, stunted and dwarfish.

'OH', my practical and somewhat sceptical husband, looms over the seedlings and pronounces their fate. 'Nasty looking things, aren't they? Bet they grow up to be something spiky.'

I understand his concern – our new allotment, nicknamed The Voodoo Plot for its gloomy appearance and sinister contents, has continued to surprise us, mainly with spikes!

A year after we took it on we are still finding things that aren't natural allotment items: the box of walking sticks belonging to dead people, discovered at the back of the potting shed, turned out to be balanced by another box of walking sticks belonging to dead people, found lurking behind the greenhouse, doubling the number of potential haunters that walk through my dreams at night; there are disembodied dolls' heads buried under plants; brass incense burners decorated with crescent moons buried in planters (burying is a constant theme, which is as worrying as anything else); and, verging on normalcy, stashes of beer and vodka bottles... the list is lengthening and not getting any less peculiar.

There have been nasty surprises of the horticultural variety too – the huge holly bush on the corner of the plot has been under-planted with a member of the *Lonerica* family that is so prickly and toxic it might as well be a tribe of Amazonian pygmies equipped with poisoned darts. It's not often that any plant gets the better of OH, who is six foot two and highly energetic, but the *Lonerica* is definitely winning the battle. Even putting our incinerator on it in November and lighting fires on top of it hasn't killed it – the old shoots burnt but it's stubbornly throwing out new ones and each time OH tries to remove the hideous shrub, he comes home covered in scratches that itch and refuse to heal.

Inspired by Celia's dedication, in fear of her wrath, and intimidated by the seedlings, I spend more time in my own greenhouses than ever before, trying to avoid failure in my own germination process.

20 March

OH leaves the early greenhouse weeks to me, as he has an aversion to thinning seedlings. Today I am thinning with a vengeance. For big bruiser seedlings like cucurbits I plant two seeds to a self-watering propagator (see May) and when both have germinated I simply nip the weaker of the two between my finger and thumbnails at soil level and leave the stronger to grow on for a week or so before repotting.

For tiny surface-sown seedlings like the ones I am working on today I use a brilliant device – a pair of angled chiropody scissors. With them I can shear the unwanted, weaker seedlings just above the soil to give plenty of growing space to the stronger specimens, without the risk of damaging neighbouring plants. Something in me becomes mischievous – perhaps it's the added warmth of the greenhouse making my blood overheat – but instead of carefully removing every other seedling so that each baby plant has a chance to grow unimpeded, I come over all creative and cut the tiny swathe so that it resembles a heart. I step back to admire my handiwork, which is like a doll's house topiary, and only then do I realise I've just sculpted away half our leek seedlings, and guiltily rush down to the shop to buy another packet of seeds and sow them in the hope that by the time I must confess to OH what I have done, there will be a second sowing ready to be thinned.

22 March

Celia rings daily for a report on her miserable-looking whatever-they-ares. She won't tell me what genus and variety I'm raising, because, 'You'll be intimidated.'

I concur, preferring her to believe that I would struggle to live up to the pedigree of the whatever-they-ares than to tell the truth: I probably wouldn't recognise them from their botanical name and even if she told me the common one I'd almost certainly still fail to be intimidated because I would have absolutely no idea what they were or why they mattered.

I looked up *Tillandsias* and discovered they are a bromeliad, aka 'air plant', which, while resistant to most forms of neglect when mature, is almost impossible to raise from seed and can take up to eight years to become big enough to be considered ready to transplant! My respect for my friend increases and my fear of the Dickensian seedlings increases too, until I am getting up in the middle of the night to check on them for fear that they might be sitting in a fatal chill.

30 March

The seedlings are 4 inches tall and have two sets of true leaves – quite long leaves they are too – so I ring Celia. She is out and Stefan, her long-suffering husband, informs me that 'she may be some time'. This should ring big alarm bells but I am so desperate to be rid of the leafy invalids that I announce I'm coming round in ten minutes, strap them back into the passenger seat and drive to Celia and Stefan's house where I deposit them on the kitchen table and heave a sigh of relief.

Stefan, on the other hand, looks beleaguered and now I am free of my horticultural obligation I can relax and sympathise.

'What's up?' I say.

'Celia is being voted on today,' he says mournfully.

'Voted on?'

'She is up for election as Chair of The Exotics.'

I whistle. The Exotics is a small group of horticultural... well, the word I want to use is pedants but Celia would probably say they are experts or devotees. We might compromise on divas, I suppose. The Exotics raise unusual (some would say impossible) plants from seed and have arcane competitions. I remember meeting the winner of 'who can grow the biggest banana plant in five years from seed' and wondering first why anybody would take part in a five-year-long competition, second whether the dedication to the cause had led to the gentleman's complete abandonment of social niceties such as bathing and third how on earth he'd managed to live to the end of the five-year process when I wanted to murder him after just six minutes in his company. Similar contests have led to long arguments in the quarterly newsletter of The Exotics which is usually one page of events, and seven pages of letters in which the members assassinate each other's characters, sometimes in Latin! There have also been a couple of brawls after the Annual Dinner at which a trophy is awarded to the most accomplished grower. Well, supposedly it is – usually the committee say nobody has met the strict criteria which include, for example, growing *Encephalartos woodii*, the world's rarest tree, extinct in the wild, which doesn't produce seeds and therefore has to be grafted! To me, this all sounds a little excessive and socially unattractive.

Celia, on the other hand, finds The Exotics stimulating. Obviously so, as she is trying to become the putative leader of this bunch of malcontent plant worshippers.

'So what have I been growing?' I gesture at the Dickensians as they lounge in their pots like tuberculosis sufferers heading for a consumptive decline.

Stefan squints at them, clearly as unenthused by their appearance as I am. '*Drosophyllum lusitanicum*,' he says, 'also known as dewy pine.'

I squint at the seedlings. 'They don't look like a pine.'

'They aren't. They're carnivorous.' He picks up the pots and stows them in the conservatory and I head for home, glad to be free of the things and convinced that from the beginning I knew they were killers.

Celia rings at nine to tell me she has been voted in. She sounds exultant and I try to be excited. When she suggests I attend a committee meeting though, I remind her of my plebeian horticultural background and am glad to be let off. The idea of spending time with more than one Exotic is terrifying. I would be egging the dewy pine onto them in no time.

Healthy greenhouse seedlings

Greenhouse seedlings should be looking vigorous by now. Assuming you check your seedlings daily for moisture, pests and signs of distress – plus regularly turning pots or trays – you're giving your plants an excellent chance of being sturdy. After many years of losing tender seedlings we've formulated some simple rules to avoiding sickly greenhouse germination:

Temperature – it's important to keep an eye on your greenhouse temperatures. Few of us have a problem with temperatures too high in January and February, but it can happen that the temperature soars in March – all it takes is a sunny day or two, especially if you have a greenhouse heater too. This can lead to the plants shooting upwards, thinking it is much later in the year and that they need to grow rapidly to 'catch up'. It leads to long spindly plant stems and if the temperature drops again, the shock to the system can kill the new plants. A maximum/minimum thermometer and a careful eye on the suggested temperatures for germination will help you to avoid such problems.

Light – low light levels make early seedlings stretch towards what little light is available, which can leave them spindly and weak, and even lead to them collapsing and dying when they are planted out. Many hobby growers now use 'growlights' or daylight balanced bulbs to give precious plants 16 hours of 'daylight' in every 24. If you're not up for that, planting large seeds with a layer of white vermiculite over the top can double the light that hits the seedlings. Having mirrors in your greenhouse (but not right next to the seedlings, or they might fry) also increases light levels, as does painting woodwork white and setting white polystyrene tiles on the staging so that light is reflected back to the plants from below their pots or trays. This is where turning pots or trays is valuable: I now grow all our seeds in square or round containers, rather than rectangular, so that they can be turned through 90 degrees each morning, giving them a four-day rotation back to the beginning – it seems to keep the stems shorter and stronger than turning through 180 degrees as is often necessary for longer trays on narrower staging or windowsills.

Air movement – commercial growers of tender crops use fans to blow gentle zephyrs of greenhouse temperature air across their seedlings. This encourages them to grow shorter and stronger stems. Most of us don't have the capacity or desire to engineer a gentle greenhouse breeze, but it's a good idea to move your hand over the top of your seedlings when they are about four to six weeks old, just for a few seconds daily and just strongly enough to move the top growth slightly, as this has the same effect at a much lower level of intensity. Ensuring you thin seedlings and don't pack pots and containers into every available corner of your staging will also help prevent the dreaded damping-off fungus, which runs rife if air circulation is poor.

Depth – read seed packets carefully or ask other growers if you have obtained 'swap' or saved seeds that didn't come with horticultural guidelines. A seed set too deep in the soil will use up most of its energy in reaching the surface, and may then expire from exhaustion. The same effect happens if the planting medium is too firm, so don't *press* the compost down on top of the seeds and when you water, don't allow the water to hit the soil surface too heartily, as this can compact the crust, which, as it dries, becomes difficult for the new growth to penetrate. Seeds have a finite amount of energy, held in the cotyledon (or seed embryo) which creates the first leaves that push through the soil to reach the air. If the energy in the cotyledon is exhausted by the journey, it can be too weak to create the rest of the system (embryonic roots and the conversion cells to convey nutrients from the soil and move them around the plant) that allows the seed to become a viable plant. This is what happens when we see the first leaves appear but within a couple of days the plantlet just expires for no apparent reason.

Nutrients – either too rich a soil, or too poor a one, can kill seedlings. As soon as the first true (non-cotyledon) leaves appear, it is time to move the plants from their potting medium, or to give them a very week nutrient feed such as a seaweed solution. Potting compounds like John Innes No. 2 are great to germinate seeds, but not rich enough to keep seedlings going for more than a couple of weeks, so be ready to pot on into something richer. Rich compost can also cause seedlings to fail. Some composts are enriched with granular fertiliser and this can cause seedlings to become big, green and sappy – they look great but the cell walls in such seedlings are too big and fragile to cope with outdoor conditions and the plants flop over when they are potted on or planted out. Getting the seed compost right is more than fussiness – it can determine the future of the plant. Read packets carefully and ask other growers for advice.

Factor in the hardening-off process – take, as an example, the supersweet corns such as Lark, Butterscotch or Earlibird. The reason I don't start them before March, even in a greenhouse, is that if you look at the commercial growing instructions (usually much more detailed than the amateur seed packet information and often readily available online through horticultural/agricultural college websites) it suggests that for supersweets to set good cobs, they need to be planted out in soil of 21°C once they've germinated. They are never going to get that, consistently, in the UK, but we can try to give them the best start possible. For many years I started them in February, and they became tall and leggy by the time it was safe to plant them out in May and didn't produce many cobs! If I planted them outside earlier in the year to stop them getting leggy, say in April, they also failed to produce cobs! So when planning the germination of crops that will eventually be planted outdoors, count forwards to the optimum time to plant the seeds out, and then sow them the recommended period of days (plus or minus seven) back from that optimum planting-out date.

Sowing and growing

- Early **Brussels sprouts**, if started now in a seed bed and given ample time to establish, can be ready by mid September (of course, you have to be the kind of person who wants to eats sprouts in mid September for this to be an appealing idea!).
- **Summer cabbage, leeks** and **cauliflowers** can be sown in seed beds with some protection both above (fleece or similar) and alongside (March winds hitting plant stems will kill as many tender seedlings as frost). This is where seed beds, nursery beds or raising plants in trays in a cold frame can be the ideal solution for those who like to get plants started early.

- Early **peas** can be planted now, but only if you can keep them frost free, either in a greenhouse or under a substantial frost cover – horticultural fleece alone is not usually enough to get peas through to April without their growth being checked by a temperature drop.

- **Lettuce, radish, spring onions, carrots, beetroot,** early **parsnips** and **turnips** can all be sown in open ground – you may need to use cloches or fleece to protect seedlings on most nights this month.

- **Onions** for storing, whether from sets or seed, can go in the ground in March in mild areas, April for harsh climates. Onion sets are like miniature onions, which is in fact what they are – somebody else has done the hard work of raising them from seed so they can make lots of growth as soon as they reach the soil. They should be sown in a light soil – scrape a little dip to pop your sets into, pointy end up, or sow your seeds in tiny depressions in the soil. Give them 15 centimetres between sets or seeds to get full-size onions, 10–12 centimetres if you want smaller ones. If planting sets, remember to cover them, or stretch string between them, to stop birds pecking them up. Bigger sets are more likely to bolt (flower) than small ones, so sow the smallest first as they are most likely to produce a good onion. You can sow onion seed in trays to plant out, but my experience is that they tend to bolt. Always remember which onions you're planting – spring-sown seed or spring sets can be stored for months, maybe right up until the next year's autumn sets are ready, but autumn-planted sets only keep until the beginning of winter.

- **Peppers** and **chillies, tomatoes,** indoor **cucumbers** and supersweet **sweetcorn** can all be sown in a greenhouse.

Crop care and allotment tasks

Many people will be planting their **onions** and **shallots** in a dry March, but if the weather is very damp, it's often best to hold off until April.

Around mid March is best to start off your first early **potatoes**, if you're able to keep them frost free, and **Jerusalem artichokes** often perform best when planted now.

This is also the time of year to think about starting a new **asparagus** bed from crowns – I covered establishing an asparagus bed, and good varieties to grow, in *Minding My Peas and Cucumbers*.

Fruit trees, if bare-rooted, can still be planted, and March is the optimum month to move or plant **raspberries**.

Finish pruning **apple** and **pear trees** if you didn't do them in January, and take old stems out of the heart of **currant** bushes, shortening side-shoots to a single bud to give an open centre to the bush so air can circulate.

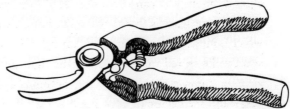

Crops to harvest

- Late **Brussels sprouts** will still be available in March, as will **winter cauliflowers**.
- **Chard** is a good leaf crop in March, and you should also be harvesting all forms of **kale**.
- **Endive** is still edible if you kept it going through the winter under fleece or cloches but if you forced it, this is just the time to break the last of the delicious heads from the roots and enjoy a feast!
- **Leeks** you've left in the ground over the winter can be lifted now and used up in soups and stews.
- **Pak choi** and **mizuna** grown in a cold greenhouse will be welcome additions to the March food table, given that this is part of the hungry gap – the period before the spring vegetables are ready, but the winter vegetables have either been eaten or become inedible through drying out, rotting or starting to produce shoots in preparation for another year of growing. **Winter density lettuce** is readily available from a winter sowing too.
- **Parsnips** need to be lifted or they will try to become perennials by putting out new growth, which means the inner core of the root becomes woody and unpleasant to eat. In the 'soft south' we are often harvesting our first **purple sprouting** this month, so keep checking yours to see if it's ready.
- **Rhubarb** is ready, especially if you forced it, whether indoors or out.

- **Savoy cabbages** with their tough outer leaves should still be good after even the worst winter, but the slugs will be trying to eat them too.
- **Swedes** can be harvested if they were left in the ground – while they don't go woody, they can turn dry and fibrous if they start to put on spring growth.
- **Wild garlic** (**ramsons**) may just be ready in March in the south but please don't harvest it from the wild – plants can be bought from many herb suppliers and they multiply rapidly if planted in a shady area (ours grow in the hedge and under the raspberries and get culled regularly or they'd take over the plot!).

Recipe of the month:

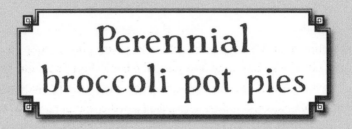

Perennial broccoli pot pies

At this time of year, allotment workers require a substantial meal! It's not usually fun to be working outdoors in March.

Perennial broccoli is like an open-headed cauliflower – creamy in colour and delicate in flavour. The plant lasts three to seven years and can be harvested between February and April annually. It's ideal for a hearty pot pie and doesn't require any of that faffing around making a white sauce that usually goes with winter vegetable pies. You can ring the changes on this in a number of ways: add sweetcorn or chopped ham or top with puff pastry instead of the breadcrumbs, but I think this is the simplest, healthiest version.

Around 200 g perennial broccoli or purple sprouting broccoli or cauliflower florets
30 g butter or 25 ml olive oil
1 onion, peeled and finely chopped
A small handful of ramsons leaves, chopped, torn or shredded
100 ml milk
300 g cheese: you need three different cheeses – a mozzarella type, a cream cheese and a strong hard cheese. The proportions can vary, but you need to have at least 100 g of mozzarella for the recipe to work

Your choice of winter herbs
70 g fresh breadcrumbs, 20 g oats and around 30 g finely
grated hard cheese mixed together

Soften the cream cheese by beating it in a large bowl, chop the mozzarella if it's not grated and grate the hard cheese and add to the bowl with half the ramsons and your chosen herbs: we like thyme, winter savory and some crushed dried coriander seed.

Wash (if necessary) and steam the broccoli until al dente.

Preheat oven to 165°C/gas mark 3.

While the oven is heating, fry the onion in the butter or oil until translucent, tip into the bowl and fold the milk, broccoli and onion into the mixture.

Divide the mixture between four large oiled ramekins or small bowls, sprinkle remaining ramsons over and top with the breadcrumb and cheese mix.

Put the four dishes on a tray and bake for 15–20 minutes.

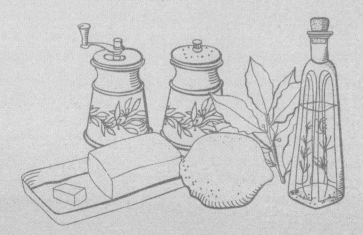

April

15 April

Have been to the Heritage seed swap, despite OH begging me not to and pointing out that we have more seeds to sow than space to sow them in, plus two greenhouses full of plants hardening off, and half an allotment full of open-sown seedlings that need watering, weeding and thinning. The thing is, I have loads of seeds to swap still, and if I didn't go I would always have wondered if there was something there, something rare and wonderful (and tasty!) that I would have missed if I hadn't been present on the day that it was offered. That's how I got my first crystal lemon cucumber seeds and the way that I obtained the soldier beans that have become a feature of our edible landscaping as well as a mainstay of our winter cuisine. Not to be there would be sacrilegious.

I adore seed swaps, although I approach them in the same half-hopeful, half-cynical spirit that a divorcee brings to online matchmaking. Most seed swaps have some kind of catering, lots of interesting stalls with aids to environmental gardening and sometimes there's even singing and dancing, and you don't get that in a garden centre!

On the other hand, though, many seed swaps have participants who either don't know what they are doing or don't understand why other people don't wish to plant their broad beans naked at the new moon (or whatever). Finding knowledgeable swappers with whom to swap is part of the fun, but it has to be done in the spirit of adventure rather than certainty – no seed from a swap should be relied upon to produce a guaranteed harvest because the recipient is dependent upon the skill, judgement and honesty of the seed saver.

I see Compact and Bijou leaving the swap as I arrive, their arms filled with swaps and purchases, their heads close together as they compare their treasures – it's like looking at Tweedledum and Tweedledee dressed by Calvin Klein and Paul Smith. They are definitely the most stylish tenants on our allotment site, if not the most horticulturally productive. The couple are so deep in conversation they don't notice me and I shiver with delighted anticipation as I notice that Bijou has a newspaper-wrapped parcel under his arm, out of which is sticking a black-painted plaster boot. It's bound to be another gnome to add to his large and somewhat X-rated collection and it will probably give their allotment neighbours an apoplexy. When Compact and Bijou find yet another way to kitsch up their allotment, the fallout is like watching a shed-based version of *Big Brother* – I feel guilty about enjoying it, but it's brilliantly entertaining. Anybody who thinks allotments are boring clearly hasn't experienced the fireworks that result from one allotment-holder getting right up another allotment-holder's nose!

16 April

I have bargains and rarities from the seed swap that I want to brag about so I head for the allotment site, where I can be sure of finding people who will envy my haul.

It's a nasty rainy day and I have to hunt around to find somebody to show off to, but eventually I find Maisie sitting in her shed – with the kettle on, which is a bonus – and lay out my envelopes, paper bags and little plastic packets of seed. Celia would be horrified by the plastic sachets: she considers it herbicide to put any potential plant inside plastic which, she claims, is a prime cause of faulty or failed germination.

Maisie is not as thrilled as I had expected. She listens as I explain all the wonderful things I have obtained, and what I swapped for each one (a seed swapper can be just as boring as a fisherman when it comes to stories) and then, when I fall silent, she stirs her tea, dunks a biscuit and announces, 'I'm giving up my plot in November.'

For a moment I think I've misheard. Maisie's roots, literally, run deep in our site. Her grandfather and father had the plot before her, and she's one of our proudest stalwarts. The plum tree on her plot was planted by her father and the path was built by her grandfather – she must be pulling my leg.

'Jim's brassica disease is worse. I'm giving up the plot and we're going on a cruise, then, when we get back, he's going to have an operation.'

I process this information through my Maisie filter. Brassica disease is vascular disease and Mr Maisie's difficulties with this condition have been a part of her conversation for quite a few years, but this sounds like a worsening situation.

'I'm sorry to hear it, but didn't the doctor tell him he needed to eat lots of healthy food and take lots of exercise? Well, your allotment provides the healthy food and if he came up here more often, he'd get more exercise, surely?' I gaze at her hopefully.

Maisie nods. 'Yes, but Jim doesn't like the allotment and he says

I've given enough time to it. If we want to make the most of our lives, we need to do some of the things we've been putting off: a trip to the Caribbean, then his op, then we're going to take up ballroom dancing, crown-green bowling, bell-ringing and wine-of-the-month club.' She nods again, agreeing with herself. 'It's time I stopped pulling the wool over the bushel – Jim's been very patient with me and now he wants my company he's going to get it. I've already told the committee my plot will be vacated in November.'

I cannot sway her. I leave, discreetly depositing a packet of black coat runner bean seeds under my chair. My words may have little effect on Maisie, but I'm sure she'll respond to the challenge of a rare variety. It's too late to sow the seed with any guarantee of success this year, so I'm quietly confident that she'll find herself keeping the plot for just one more year, for the sake of the black coats.

22 April

Celia rings. 'Are you willing to help me organise something noteworthy for my first meeting as Chair of The Exotics?'

I visualise feeding the current Treasurer of The Exotics (a man for whom the term dour could have been coined) to a giant *Drosophyllum lusitanicum* and, as a result, probably express more enthusiasm than is sensible.

'Good,' she says. 'Then would you please organise a buffet for the thirty-four expected attendees, which will feature vegetables and other produce from each of the continents.'

'Antarctica?' I wail. 'What vegetables are there from Antarctica?'

'Seaweeds,' she replies briskly and hangs up.

As is so often the case with my friend, I find myself staring at the phone with a feeling of panic-stricken awe. Celia always knows what she wants, it's just a question of who's going to get it for her... and once again, the getting seems to be my responsibility.

29 April

I'm showing new allotment-holders how to tackle some of the things that are so blithely described in gardening books. The 'Grow and Tell' classes I run every year are designed to help people master basic tasks that are rarely explored in depth but are fundamental to successful year-round growing. Soil warming, for example: just about every allotment book says that soil warming is a good idea but how, and why?

Today's lesson is conducted with two meat thermometers, two notebooks and a bunch of enquiring minds. OH and I prepared the test beds ten days ago: black polythene over one patch of soil, horticultural fleece over another, fleece laid on top of grass clippings on a third. The students divide into two groups, to see if they get the same results, then they lift the cover at each end of the test bed, and record the ambient temperature and the soil temperatures at around 3 centimetres and 6 centimetres deep. They also look at other things: the compaction of the soil, the dampness, the rate of weed seed germination...

By and large, what they conclude is that soil-warming for seed germination entails a lot of effort and the return may be limited. Weed seeds definitely love it, which is one problem, and the different forms of warming device all have advantages and disadvantages. Black plastic leads to dry soil and as soon as you water it, the soil ends up the same temperature as the water, so what's the point? You could try to keep the water warmer than the standard soil temperature, but it's a lot of effort.

Horticultural fleece makes a degree or so of temperature difference, which is great, but at 6 centimetres the soil is exactly the same temperature as uncovered soil, so when the seeds get their roots down to that depth, which they do pretty quickly, given the perfect conditions in which they've germinated until that point, they receive a check to their growth and seeds planted in un-warmed soil often catch up over the growing season as a result of that shock to the system.

Fleece plus a hot bed of grass clippings makes 3–4°C of difference. Phenomenal! Almost tropical! Of course, when you brush away the grass clippings it's obvious that the weed seeds just love those few degrees of heat and would definitely be outcompeting any refined, wimpy, demanding crop seed that somebody might have chosen to sow in the same spot.

So, more often than not, the students come to the conclusion that I reached long ago. Soil warming needs to be undertaken much earlier than books suggest, like around January. It needs to be done on well-weeded, regularly hoed, reasonably irrigated soil and it needs to be maintained – which means raised beds. And at that point they become very interested in how OH makes our raised beds, because it's obvious that's the way to go. So I step back and have a quick cup of allotment tea while he takes them through the process of nails and wood and hammers and glue… sometimes it's good to know your limitations and carpentry is mine!

Running a successful seed swap

Make sure you have enough seeds of your own to start the swap – you can do this by inviting along people who are good seed savers, and by saving your own seed throughout the year to make a good stock.

Instead of having people sit at their own tables, with their own seed, label tables with plant families: roots, salad leaves, squashes and pumpkins, peas and beans, fruit, flowers, herbs, etc. As people arrive, get them to move around the inside circle of the tables, putting down all the swap packets they have brought and then invite them to move back to the outside circle to browse for seeds they'd like to take home. This encourages sharing and chatting and getting to know other growers.

Get loads of publicity – and make sure that everybody is welcome by using a slogan like 'come along even if you don't have swaps, you can take home a sample packet to get started', and then have some really simple seeds (radish, lettuce, nasturtiums) in small packets with good cultivation notes, to give to newcomers who might be nervous about growing from seed.

Put up some posters suggesting that people swap as many packets as they brought and that in the last hour of the swap, all remaining seeds will be 'homed' in a free auction. Get a knowledgeable grower to stand up and name each available seed packet, saying a couple of words about the plant, and then invite those present to raise their hands if they want the seed. When they get a packet they move to the back so people who haven't got a 'free' packet of seed are at the front.

Offer some simple talks – keeping them to five minutes. Good subjects are:

- 'How to save seed' – a simple description of seed-saving will help people to save more viable seed and to share it. Showing them how to record what and when they harvest and keep track of the age of the seed allows many growers to develop a whole new area of activity and to save money too.
- 'Why you can't save seed from hybrid plants' – a lot of people don't understand the F1 hybrid system and will have brought along swap seeds that won't come true to variety. If you run this talk at the beginning, they might remove those seeds from their swap pile and save another grower a lot of confusion.
- 'How long can seed be saved?'– if you print off a simple list of seed viability as found in many seed company catalogues, it's easy to give a five-minute talk on the different timescales and then direct people to a poster on the wall to check the viability of their own seed.

Remember that people may have their own good ideas – perhaps they want to create a cooperative to split seed packets between them or a 'grow to cook' group where people with gardens grow ingredients for cooks who don't have gardens and who then give part of their cooked dishes back to the gardener. Maybe they want to learn to pickle vegetables or make wine: an ideas board where people can pin up their wishes and see who else might be keen to get involved can create communities of interest way outside of just growing stuff!

Invite local farmers, brewers, bakers, restaurants and fishermen along... people who like to grow their own flowers, fruit and veg often want to eat and buy more local produce and to contribute to their community. Being inclusive can make an event more exciting and spread the load placed on you, the organiser, to make things a success.

Sowing and growing

If March was harsh, April may be an intense sowing month when you have to get everything in the ground in a hurry, so be ready! This month you can sow:

- Beetroot
- Broccoli
- Brussels sprouts
- Cabbage
- Cauliflower
- Chard

- **French beans** – with frost protection
- **Kale**
- **Kohlrabi** – with frost protection
- **Leeks**
- **Peas**
- **Rocket** and **lettuce** – with frost protection
- **Spinach** – with frost protection
- **Sweetcorn** – with frost protection
- **Salsify** and **scorzonera** like the same kind of soil as carrots: light, friable (i.e. easy to break up and crumble), stone-free and they also grow as long roots. The difference between the two plants, superficially, is the size of their leaves. Salsify has skinny, frilly looking leaves while those of scorzonera are broader and more substantial. The significant difference is that scorzonera is a perennial so if it's not bulked up by the first autumn, you can leave it in the ground for another year, while salsify, treated the same way, will simply bolt, run up to flowers and be inedible. Both taste like parsnips crossed with asparagus to me, although the classic flavour definition is oyster-like. The roots are black, so don't panic when you harvest your first crop and they come out like coal-dust-covered carrots. Both roots can be peeled before cooking or the black skin can be rubbed away once they have been cooked.
- **Aubergines, celery** and **celeriac** and outdoor **cucumbers** can all be sown in the greenhouse this month, as can **cantaloupe melons** – set two seeds on edge in a pot in a heated propagator or on a sunny windowsill and pinch out the weakest seedling when they have their first leaves. These are good seeds to sow in a plant-and-leave propagator too.

- If you started **lemongrass** earlier in the year, and it's established a good root system, this is the time to move it into a 15-centimetre pot in the greenhouse, with a layer of gravel in the base for good drainage and another layer on the top, to ensure moisture is retained where needed. It is a grass, and it loves humidity but hates too much direct sun, strong wind or waterlogged soil so give it a water spray every couple of days, as well as bottom-watering the pot.

Crop care and allotment tasks

This is the time of year to plant out both kinds of **artichokes: globe** and **Jerusalem**. Globe artichokes, from seed, should be sown in a seed bed, with two or three seeds going into each station (a station is a dip or declivity in the soil) around 30 centimetres between stations. Thin once the first rounded leaves appear (before the first true leaves, which are longer with jagged edges) to leave just the strongest seedling in each station. Transplant them to their permanent home when the plants have five true leaves and protect seedlings from

slugs and snails as they are very prone to damage in their first few months of life. Water well until established. Jerusalems are even easier – they are grown from tubers, so simply plant them around 12 centimetres deep and 30 centimetres apart in prepared soil. If you want good big tubers, you'll need to either stake them, or cut off the flower heads in summer, to stop wind rock loosening the roots and keeping the tubers small, but most people don't bother and still get more than enough tubers to keep them going through the winter.

Onions and **shallot** sets can be planted out now, especially if you live in an area where March planting is too risky – check your last frost dates and cover the sets with fleece if there's any risk. You may also need to protect them from birds, which like to peck them out of the ground – we prefer putting down chicken-wire cloches as opposed to the stick-with-string-wound-round approach which (a) has been known to trip up Rebus the cairn terrier, (b) often gets gnawed through by mice and (c) doesn't stop the local fox using our lovely onion bed as a toilet – she just picks her way between the string and dumps anyway!

New **asparagus** crowns are best planted after your last frost date in April.

Potatoes are usually planted around April. Traditionally allotment-holders would plant their spuds in Easter week, partly because the mandatory holiday gave working men a couple of days of leisure to get to the plot and do the heavy work of potato planting. We dig trenches and in the bottom strew a mixture of a third each of chopped comfrey, grass clippings from the first lawn cut of the year, and soil taken from the trench. This provides nutrition for the potatoes, which are a hungry crop, and also gives moisture to the tuber as it starts to grow, reducing the need for watering in the early weeks.

Crops to harvest

- **Asparagus** if you're lucky with the weather and have grown an early variety like Gijnlim.
- **Cabbages**
- **Cauliflower**
- **Chard**
- Overwintered **squashes**: if you harvested storing squashes in October and November then this is the month to use them up – and don't just think pumpkin soup! Roasted with fresh herbs or made into a rich flan with a robust cheese and leek mixture, squashes add interest and substance to a month when home-grown food is limited in availability.
- **Perpetual spinach**
- **Purple sprouting broccoli**
- We'll also be using up the last of the dried **beans** from the previous year. Usually we have **borlotti beans** and either **soldier beans** or **Cherokee Trail of Tears** which we grow and dry for use through the winter. Pulses you raise yourself are larger and tastier than shop ones, but should be used within 12 months of drying or they start to lose flavour and become tough.

- These are the last weeks of the hungry gap, when growers start staring hungrily at the new season's crops, trying to hurry them into readiness through willpower! Plants that bridge the gap, like **herbs** that have been started in the greenhouse, are a valuable addition to otherwise boring meals. We usually enjoy **basil**, early **chervil** grown from seed that can have a few leaves harvested by now, and substantial crops of **chives** that we potted up in autumn and brought indoors, along with greenhouse overwintered **French tarragon**. If we were lucky with germination, we may even have some early **flat leaf parsley** to add to our meals.

Recipe of the month:

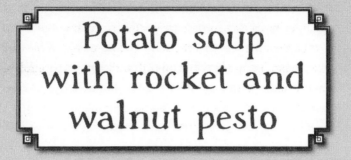

Potato soup with rocket and walnut pesto

Potato soup doesn't sound exciting, but made with the first new potatoes (usually those raised in containers under cover) and the first of the rocket, it's really tasty! It can either be made in the slow cooker or on the hob.

1 kg new potatoes, well scrubbed but not peeled and cut into
1.5-cm cubes
1 large onion, finely chopped
4 cloves garlic
800 ml vegetable or chicken stock
75 g cream cheese (softened by beating it in a bowl before using)
Sprig rosemary
Bay leaf

For the slow cooker: just put the potatoes, onion, garlic, herbs and stock in the slow cooker, stir well together and cook on high for six hours or on low for ten.

On the hob, gently fry the onion in a tablespoon of olive oil, then stir in the garlic, herbs and potatoes with the stock and cook for 20–30 minutes.

For both recipes, just before serving, add the cream cheese and stir together, then remove half the soup and puree it in a blender before recombining and serving topped with a big spoonful of rocket and walnut pesto.

Pesto

50 g walnut pieces
3 tbsp olive oil
1 tbsp walnut oil
1 garlic clove, peeled and minced
2 large handfuls rocket leaves, large ribs removed, washed and dried
30 g grated parmesan
Seasoning

Dry fry the walnut pieces gently until they become aromatic, then tip them into a blender with the rocket leaves, garlic and parmesan and pulse gently. Continue to blend, pouring the oils into the top until you get a smooth pesto. Taste and adjust seasoning – if your rocket is very young it may be sufficiently peppery and more mature parmesan is often salty enough not to need any more salt.

This pesto is also good in baked potatoes or used in sandwiches.

May

9 May

I'm not usually at the plot every day, but greenhouse seedlings are diva-like in their needs and May is the month when I spend nearly every lunch break at The Voodoo Plot, tending to their outrageous demands. By June most greenhouse crops are well established enough to need only a mid-week visit, maybe more if it's very hot and dry, but in May they expire if you so much as glance at them sideways.

Bijou appears in the distance, moving fast. I know it's him because of his extremely natty hat ('Genuine Panama dahling, nothing but the best for *me*!') but the speed at which he's travelling makes me squint. I've seen Compact and Bijou beetling rapidly around before now, but always on their way home ('Pimm's and a foot bath for me, dahling, I've absolutely *wrecked* my hands picking and weeding – slave labour, that's what it is!'), so this swift progress towards the plot is unheard of. About 50 metres behind is Compact, wearing what I privately call his Land Admiral's cap. It's jaunty, has gold braid and a visor and is nothing like what most allotment-holders consider suitable attire. He could definitely launch a thousand ships wearing it, although whether the sailors could stop laughing long enough to navigate is another question. Compact is strolling, stopping to peer over fences and generally putting on a pantomime of being in no hurry.

Intrigued by their behaviour, I drift to the bottom of The Voodoo Plot, then out of the gate as if admiring my own hedge, and then towards the water tank, cleverly arriving at the junction of the paths just as Compact does.

'What's up?' I say, indicating his rapidly disappearing partner.

'Can't imagine what you're talking about. I don't see anybody.' He puts his chin up and stares directly at Bijou's back.

'Oh. OK. Well… everything OK?' I am flummoxed by this response and it shows.

'I'm fine, dear. Never been better. If you're asking me about other people, well… I will let *them* speak for themselves.' And off he goes, stalking slowly past each plot like an allotment inspector with a zeal for the job.

16 May

Felix has no visible means of support but many invisible ones. His income derives from the stock market, or so he tells us, augmented by some 'projects' which are never clearly defined but which have included selling 'antiques', buying wine in South America and importing it to sell to restaurants here, and a chi-chi veg box scheme in which he supplied the lonely housewives of Sussex with *bouquets garnis* and a level of personal attention that seemed to infuriate their husbands.

This peculiar lifestyle means that Felix is on his allotment from dawn until dusk, and quite often after. He has a light that runs off a car battery, a clockwork radio and a preference for beer at ambient temperature that allows him to spend many evenings communing with nature in his shed. It also means that he knows everything about everybody in our community, so it was to Felix I headed in order to discover what was going on with Compact and Bijou, our previously happiest couple.

From quite a distance away I could see him, stooping over some allotment task and when he straightened and fixed me with his bright blue eyes I had to remind myself to be on my guard. Felix looks like the sweetest, most innocent, naive man you could ever meet. His tanned open face, broad smile, rolling Sussex accent and slow demeanour all combine to give the impression that he's a throwback to an earlier, more innocent generation who tilled the soil and were content to live a simple life. Nothing could be further from the truth: Felix is the biggest rogue around, always trying to get something for nothing, and constant exposure to his schemes and snares has taught me caution.

'What's up with Compact and Bijou?' I ask.

'It's an issue of artichokes from the seed swap,' Felix tells me.

'Ah...' I understand immediately. 'Globe or Jerusalem?'

'Jerusalem.'

'Compact or Bijou?'

'Compact.'

'Ah ha.' I am now fully informed.

The problem with Jerusalem artichokes is that you can eat them or you can't – it's not a question of liking them, it's one of tolerance. And if you are the one who finds Jerusalem artichokes disagreeable, then even a small amount of that knobbly tuber in a meal can give you an intensely uncomfortable and embarrassing evening. On the other hand, if you like them (and they like you) they can become a real fixation. Rather like garlic fanatics, Jerusalem-lovers think their favoured food adds a little something to most dishes. And when one of you enjoys Jerusalems and the other doesn't, it can be a divisive issue, in both culinary and horticultural terms.

As crops, Jerusalems are pretty to look at and ridiculously easy to grow. Most allotment novices seize on them with joy, as they fill a large area, require almost no work and crowd out many kinds of weed. Of course, five years later, when they are digging stray Jerusalems out of their strawberry bed they may not be so enthused, but that's part of the process of learning how to manage an allotment.

Armed with my new knowledge, I wander up to Compact and Bijou's plot and discover, as I had anticipated, that a large bed has been prepared. It runs along their front fence and Compact is standing beside it, with a crumpled paper bag in his hand. Bijou is in the shed but he's remonstrating with his partner at a decibel level that can be heard halfway across the site.

'How *can* you? I mean really… what kind of a person *are* you? Isn't it enough that you get your way about the chandeliers, and the pyjamas and the dogs… must you inflict your disgusting root vegetables on me too?'

Compact takes his admiral's stance and declaims, 'Your problem, Benjamin, is that you think the world revolves around you. Why shouldn't I grow my favourite vegetables, which, by the way, are not at all disgusting, when more than half this plot is given over to your pathetic foibles?' He points dramatically to a hand-painted ceramic cherub sitting on a toadstool, perhaps overdramatically, as the knobbly Jerusalem artichokes fly out of the bag all over the ground at his feet.

Bijou laughs somewhat hysterically from the shed, putting me in mind of the old woman in *Hansel and Gretel* who laughs as she shuts the children in the oven, and I am about to creep away, sorry to have heard this discord, when Compact, scrabbling after his tubers, kicks backwards and catches the cherub with the somewhat stacked heel of his shoe (he's not nicknamed Compact for nothing) and knocks off one of its iridescent wings.

The howl from within the shed is pure maniac, and as I back away I see Bijou rush out, pull the statuette from the ground (trampling quite a few early carrots in the process) and belabour his partner with it. I think it is best for me to forget I saw any of this, so I head the long way round to get back to The Voodoo Plot, in case Felix spots me and asks me how they are getting on.

Plant-and-go-away-for-a-week propagators and how to make them

These are my favourite toys, for three reasons:
1. They recycle an otherwise largely useless plastic object
2. They allow us to plant seeds and go away for a week, without worry
3. They are fun to make!

The wick conveys water so you can be quite reckless about abandoning your plants for seven days or more, and as long as you don't fill to the top with soil, the clear plastic rim creates a nice warm, breeze-free microclimate that supports squashes, pumpkins and cucumbers for their first few days of growth – after that they crawl out of the planter and take over the windowsill, so hearty are they!

You need:
- 1.5-litre or 2-litre fizzy drink or water bottle
- Cotton-based string
- Indelible pen
- Compost
- Seeds

Method:
Take bottle and cut roughly in half, ensuring the base half is slightly taller than the top (cap) half.

Drill a hole in the lid, big enough to take a doubled cotton-rich string about 40 centimetres long – I have seen it said you can do this with a hammer and a screwdriver. Don't! You will damage the screwdriver and possibly yourself. If you don't have a drill, use an oven glove to hold a skewer in a gas flame until it is hot enough to melt plastic and then poke it through the lid. Do not use the skewer on the barbecue afterwards.

Label the top half of the bottle by turning it so the lid is down and writing on the upper edge what the propagator is going to contain.

Make a knot in the string. Insert the string into the hole in the lid so that a couple of inches of the loop stick out through the lid with the knot sitting inside the lid.

Fill the upper half of the bottle with soil, pulling the loop of string to the centre so it runs up through the compost/potting medium.

Place the bottom part of the bottle underneath and half fill with water, then drape the loose ends of string into the water. Sow two seeds in the soil. (If you are using cucurbits, for which these propagators are particularly good, sow the seed edge on so it doesn't rot.) If you forgot to label the container earlier (as I always do!), label it now.

Water each planter well from the top on the first occasion and give it a nice tap to ensure any air pockets inside the soil collapse so the 'wick' can convey water easily.

Set in a sunny place and watch the seedlings thrive!

When the first true leaves appear, nip the weaker of the two seedlings off at soil level with your fingernails or scissors to give the other all the soil nutrients. Don't pull the seedling out of the soil as you risk disturbing the roots of the one you want to continue growing.

Sowing and growing

There are loads of crops to sow outdoors now but remember, depending on where you live, a late frost may still be a possibility. May frosts are usually light air frosts so you need to have some horticultural fleece or newspaper supported on twigs or bricks or old net curtains around to cover crops if a frost is threatened. Remember to lift the frost protection the next day, or you'll be creating a dark, moist haven for every slug and snail in the territory to come and feast on your seedlings!

- **Borlotti, French, runner, wax** and **bush beans** can all be sown outdoors now.
- **Beetroot**
- **Broccoli, cabbage, kale** and **cauliflowers** can be sown in seed beds outdoors now if you didn't start them under cover last month.
- **Chicory (endive)** – about which there is a massive confusion. Chicory (often called frisée) has green leaves used in a salad and its taproot is ground and used as a stretcher for cheap brands of coffee or by those who can't drink coffee. Endive is often called 'Belgian' and has a pale, tightly furled heart which is usually blanched by covering the plant. It is eaten both cooked and raw but usually cooked. They *are* the same plant family! Look out for Belgian or blanching endive if you want to get two crops from one seed. The way to do it is to sow chicory a couple of months before your last frost date (they like a good freeze, as you'll see) and then cut-and-come-again crop the leaves from about two weeks after sowing. Lift the roots before the first

autumn frost and cut back the top growth to about 3 centimetres while trimming the roots to around 15–20 centimetres from the bulbous part of the plant. Then stand them upright in a bucket or large container with some drainage holes and pour in sand to fill all the gaps. Water. Chicory is best kept a little too wet, rather than too dry. Store somewhere cool, and keep covered. If you get them down to around zero to 3°C, they will remain dormant, but when you bring them up to 15–20°C (still keeping them covered to exclude all light) they will form dense heads of white leaves that can be cooked through the winter.

- **Kohlrabi** can be sown now. We usually start ours in pots and plant out the strongest seedlings in about a month.

- Maincrop **peas** go in the ground now.

- **Turnips** and **swedes** can be sown, remembering to thin in about 21 days and again about a month after that to get the biggest roots.

- Sow salad crops – **lettuces, radishes, spring onions** – to get succession crops. We find spring onions take longer to get going than other crops, so we start them a week before the lettuce and radish.

- Sow annual herbs like **coriander** outdoors now. It's pretty well impossible to grow leaf coriander in the UK – it always runs up to seed – but you can save the seed and use it, so it's not a wasted crop.

- We use plant-and-go-away propagators to sow **courgette**, **marrow** and **pumpkin** and put the bottles on the kitchen windowsill to have the fun of watching the Jack's-Beanstalk-style miracle of squash propagation.

Crop care and allotment tasks

Plants started in March or April may be ready to go out now. Check your **Brussels sprouts** and **summer cabbages** and see if they can be transplanted. Remember that both seedlings are very attractive to slugs and snails so offer them some form of protection against those predators.

Red cabbages can be transplanted from late April to mid June, and are somewhat less attractive to cabbage white butterflies in my experience, although slugs and snails will still munch on them. We don't net our red cabbage against butterflies and they seem to survive. They do like sun or dappled shade, so we try to pick a prime spot for them, as they don't always heart up if the shade is too dense. Cabbages that don't 'heart' simply fail to form the dense head of tightly layered leaves that excludes rain and pests and keeps the cabbage fresh and crisp. Un-hearted cabbages can still be eaten, but the leaves will be tougher and drier and more likely to have been munched on by slugs, snails and caterpillars: they also require much more washing as grit and dirt will have penetrated to the very centre of the plant. You can also mulch them, using a brassica collar if there is brassica root fly on your site, then using untreated grass clippings in a ring outside the brassica collar. If you're lucky and don't have to protect against root fly (about half the country does, the rest doesn't), then leave around an 8-centimetre circle around the stalk of the plant bare, and lay clippings in a ring outside that.

Harden off **cantaloupes** slowly from mid to late May through to mid June – never leave them exposed if there is even a hint of a danger of frost. While they are getting used to a life (semi) outdoors, get their final location in a greenhouse, cloche or cold frame ready by giving it around a bucket of well-rotted manure or compost for each melon plant, watering well and then covering with glass or clear plastic to get the soil warmed up.

Celery and **celeriac** – we don't have much luck with celery, but celeriac seems to enjoy the clay in our soil. Check if celery is self-blanching – if not, you'll need to decide what blanching system you want to use when the plants are bigger and set your planting distances accordingly. Blanching makes the stalks paler and softer and the flavour milder. You can choose from a variety of techniques – over the years we've used old plastic plant pots with the tops cut away, we've tried boards laid along either side of a row with straw packed in between the plants, we've mulched with soil drawn up around the plant, we've tied corrugated cardboard around each plant with string – experiment and find out what works for you. Celeriac is a root, so it doesn't need so much fuss.

Leeks – if any leeks have reached the diameter of a pencil, start to plant them out by digging or dibbing a 6-inch-deep hole and dropping them in. Don't fill the hole with soil; instead, fill it with water. Over a couple of weeks the leek will expand and the soil will crumble into the hole, forming a naturally friable surrounding that the widening leek can swell into as it grows.

Crops to harvest

- **Asparagus!**
- The last of the **winter cauliflowers** should be used up this month, before they flower.
- All varieties of **kale**.
- By now you should be eating the thinnings of hardy **lettuce**, **spring onions** and **radishes**, and if you're in a warm region, you may be tucking into main crops of all three.
- **Pak choi** which was sown in a trough in the greenhouse in February will be delicious now.
- First early **potatoes** grown in containers are likely to be ready now too.
- **Purple sprouting broccoli** should be at its best.
- **Spring cabbage**

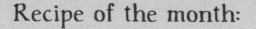

Recipe of the month:

Fisherman's parcel

We spend a lot of this month on the allotment, so food we can cook while we're there is a real joy. We have a tin lockbox in which we keep basic cooking supplies: a good cutting knife and some spoons, a couple of clean jars, a cutting board, a small bottle of olive oil and one of soy sauce, a carton of sugar, some salt and pepper – just about everything else we need is on the plot or we get creative about substitutions. The box has to be metal because rodents can smell sugar and will hunt it down in winter – for that reason too, the lockbox lives in a bigger metal box outside the shed: we don't want rats gnawing through the shed floor to try to get a sucrose fix! Because we live near the coast, good fish is easily available and OH sometimes goes line fishing and comes back with a couple of mackerel. However, if you're not a fish fan, you can make this recipe with early new potatoes instead.

2 fresh mackerel, cleaned and heads removed, or get a
fishmonger to do this for you
2 baby pak choi, sliced, or a dozen asparagus spears
2 spring onions, finely sliced
Chilli flakes – we often have a few dried chillies still hanging
onto one of last year's plants in the cold frame: to make flakes,

fold a dried chilli into tinfoil and crush but pick out the seeds
and only use the dried flaked flesh, unless you like really fiery
food!

Lemongrass – if you grow your own in a heated greenhouse,
you can simply cut a stem and slice it finely, otherwise
used dried lemongrass

Soy sauce

Oil

1 citrus fruit (orange, lemon, lime: whatever you have in the
house, or maybe greenhouse!)

Half an hour before you want to start cooking, heat a barbecue, bonfire or chimenea. Lay the fish in the centre of a large square of oiled foil and strew pak choi or asparagus, spring onions, chilli and lemongrass over the top, sliding some onion and chilli inside to flavour the flesh.

Turn up the edges of the foil before adding the next ingredients, or they will drip everywhere. Cut the citrus fruit in half and squeeze it into a jar, then tip in the soy sauce and a sprinkling of sugar if you like things sweet. Add a tablespoon of water (or wine if you happen to have some on your plot, although I can't recommend drinking and horticulture on a regular basis, it leads to pruned thumbs and raked ankles!), put the lid on the jar and shake well. Tip or spoon this over the fish and fold up the foil so the fish will steam-cook inside. There must be no gaps for the steam to escape, so we often put another layer of foil around the first parcel, to be absolutely sure.

Place on your heat source and check after 30 minutes. If it's not entirely ready, turn the fish and cook for a further ten minutes.

To cook this with potatoes, we use a variation of the classic Hasselback recipe in which slices of onion are inserted into fanned potatoes. Find two or four regularly sized potatoes (Rocket or Orla are good varieties for this) and wash well, then lay them on a secure surface and slice through almost, but not quite, to the base so that each potato has around six to eight cuts. Put the potatoes on squares of tinfoil. Into each of the cuts, drizzle a small amount of oil and then insert some pak choi or asparagus cut into suitable lengths, plus onion, lemongrass and chilli and add any fresh herbs you fancy: thyme is especially delicious. Fold up the tinfoil to make a sealed parcel and cook for 40 minutes before checking. Don't turn the potatoes over, like you did the fish, as all the goodies will fall out!

Both recipes can also be cooked in the oven at around 180°C/ gas mark 4 for around 20–25 minutes for the fish and 30–40 minutes for the spuds.

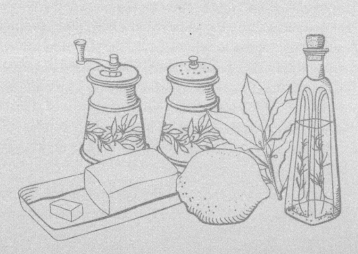

SUMMER

June

2 June

We are having a swelter: the weather went from chilly to tropical pretty well overnight. The seedlings, which were languishing and damping off in the greenhouse, all decided to expire simultaneously of sudden climate change. I've spent a long lunch break, when I should have been wrestling with an intricate article on international phishing scams, running around with buckets and screening to try to revive wilting seedlings by plunging them in cool water while rigging up sunshades for those already planted out. Several of my baby brassicas are giving the impression they have been relocated to the Sahara and one particularly fine Turk's turban squash seedling has prostrated itself across the parched earth like a citizen of Pompeii trapped by the lava.

I straighten up, exhausted, aching, and covered in the fine silt that results from trudging around with watering cans and splashing the dry earth with life-giving moisture.

OH is sitting outside the shed, looking equally jaded. He's been planting out beans. I look at my watch and realise my 'lunch break' has extended to early evening.

'Dinner?' he asks hopefully.

I would like to shrug but I cannot: my arms feel as if they have been torn from their sockets by the number of times I've walked up and down the path with cans of water. The Spanish Inquisition wasted their time contriving the strappado – they could have got their victims to irrigate their vegetable gardens and inflicted just as much pain, or so my shoulders tell me.

'Fish and chips?' I suggest and he groans. We said last year we'd never do this again: we would never, ever again end up so tired from growing food that we were too tired to cook and eat it; but here we are, once more opting for a takeaway dinner because we've used up all our energy nurturing ungrateful plants.

As we pack our tools away and try to straighten our bent backs, Felix trundles past with a wheelbarrow full of something hidden under a sack. That's not unusual: anything Felix is moving from place to place is probably illicit, underhand or ill-gotten, but there's something about his progress along the path that puzzles me and I can't quite put my finger on it.

Only when we're standing in the chip shop queue, getting dirty looks from the other customers because of our grubby appearance, does it dawn on me.

'Felix was singing something weird,' I say to OH. He doesn't reply. He's staring at the fish fryer with an expression like a starving hyena spotting a limping gazelle. I nudge him.

'Felix,' I say again. 'Humming. Today.'

OH glances at me. 'Earworm?'

For a moment I wonder if he has some kind of heat-induced derangement – perhaps a waking nightmare about some new allotment pest that he believes is savaging our plot. Then I realise he's actually been listening to me, despite his faraway gaze and a death grip on the vinegar bottle which implies that anybody getting between this man and his battered cod will rue the day.

'Oh, like the Birdie Song or Kylie Minogue you mean? No, not at all. More like… a Gregorian chant, or something Latin, anyway.'

OH snorts. 'Felix? Latin!'

I know it sounds unlikely, but that's what I heard. And then I forget all about it, in the joy of eating red-hot chips, liberally soused with vinegar, as we plod back home to rest our weary bodies. The only problem is that for the rest of the evening the earworm, 'I should be so lucky, lucky, lucky…' runs through my head on an endless loop.

5 June

The good thing about hot weather is that it limits the predators somewhat. I may be scheming against cabbage white butterflies in my dreams but at least I'm not pitting myself against slugs and snails. Then again, if it's hot enough to deter the crawlers, the red spider mite is probably causing carnage in the greenhouse – and what about ants? Some of my biggest battles in the first year on The Voodoo Plot were with ants which seemed to be a part of the overall weirdness of this neglected and peculiar bit of land – they were more aggressive than any I'd encountered before, like a plague of Egypt, confined to a single ten-rod allotment! When the world ends, I think ants will be the last thing to go.

I have had some success with removing ants from places I don't want them, but only by making the location so unpleasant for them that they up sticks to a new, usually nearby, home. Ways to deter ants include making their ant holes damp by watering around them or unstable by walloping the soil around the entry points with a sledgehammer to cause earthquakes in the tunnels below ground, but ant eradication seems to be impossible: anteaters, tapirs and echidnas probably work brilliantly but such beasts aren't native and anyway, according to wildlife programmes they have a tendency to dig that could annoy the average allotment-holder even more than ants do.

I do know a bit about this. In partnership with my determinedly dedicated horticultural friend Celia I once spent several weeks trying to find somebody with a tame echidna. It wasn't for ant-eating purposes precisely, but because Celia was trying to germinate some defiantly dormant seeds from the Australian bush. She'd contacted a specialist in bushland ecosystems who suggested (perhaps mischievously) that both Aborigines and echidnas regularly dug up bush terrain: the former for roots, the latter for ants, and that an echidna might do exactly the right kind of digging to persuade the sulky seeds to start growing. Given that the best way to germinate a large proportion of Australian plants is to expose them to smoke, or even fire – which is not the usual tender loving care bestowed on precious seeds – this seemed quite plausible, but we never managed to find an echidna to help us test the theory.

My cabbage white butterfly saga is, essentially, over. For years I fought to protect crops from the caterpillars of this elegant and yet destructive creature; now I have changed the battleground and developed a siege mentality. OH, the paragon of all things structural, has made me a brassica cage and in it, like hapless human beings facing down a horde of zombies, my few chosen brassicas live their lives in perfect peace. Constructed of wooden batten to which he has stapled horticultural netting, the cage is big enough for six cauliflowers and three purple sprouting broccoli, and that's what we intend to grow in it every year. It's also portable, so it can be moved around the plot to prevent clubroot building up in the soil. Everything else has to take its chances with the 'summer snowflakes', as cabbage whites are supposedly affectionately called (though not by any allotment-holder I've ever met), but I'm avoiding planting brightly coloured flowers next to susceptible crops like cabbages, as there is anecdotal evidence to suggest that this attracts the butterflies.

Then there are the misunderstood good guys like centipedes – a lot of people, me included, hate to come across these rapidly moving creatures but they are much more useful to the gardener than we tend to imagine. They eat loads of things we dislike: earwigs, woodlice and other annoying insects and creatures that damage plants. They also eat spiders, about which I have mixed feelings: I should like spiders because they are also beneficial to the allotment, but I haven't reached that level of sainthood yet.

Worse than any crawler, creeper or flutterer, though, are mice and rats. I'm amazed not to get more queries and complaints

about rodents when I'm teaching allotment skills, as they've been a real problem for me throughout my long and not particularly illustrious allotment career. My solution has been to acquire a terrier, and Rebus the allotment dog has a vital role to perform – at least once a week he patrols the plot, widdling on perimeter posts to remind the local foxes that this is not a good place for them to establish dens, and going into helicopter-tailed excitement if he finds a rat hole, at which point we take him home and dig half-heartedly around the location ourselves. That's usually enough to persuade the mother rat to relocate any offspring she has in the hole. It is pathetic, and we know it, but I have never wanted Rebus, or me, to dig up a nest of baby rats, so we indulge in the charade of pretend digging and hope the rodent takes the hint. Regular visits from a dog will usually discourage rats from nesting on a plot, although nothing will stop them destroying stored crops or seeds in a bad winter – they will chew through a shed wall if they are hungry enough!

7 June

Felix comes past again. This time I'm queuing to use the water tank and so I am able to stand in his way and force him to talk. Felix loves to gossip, unless he's doing something underhand, and then he prefers to pretend he's too busy to stop and chat. OH and I delight in catching him mid shenanigan and making him converse. Once again he's got a wheelbarrow full of something covered by a sack but this time I don't have to wonder what's underneath – my nose tells me. The almost ethereal fragrance of sun-ripened strawberries surrounds the barrow like a juicy aura and my mouth begins to water immediately. However, honed by years of watching Felix at work, my instincts begin to scream, 'Warning, warning!'

I put down watering cans and twitch the sack away. I have no idea what word to use for what is underneath. A mound of strawberries sounds too boring and a heap does not convey the sheer volume of fruit on display. If there were a collective noun for strawberries, it would have to be 'a magnificence' because from colour to fragrance to form, they are simply magnificent. The conversation around the water tank stops as we all stand and contemplate the small hillock of gleaming red berries.

Felix picks up the sack and drapes it back over his barrow. 'Got to get on,' he says, in a strained voice. 'Strawberries don't pick themselves, you know!'

And he's gone, trundling off down the path like the second place contestant in a wheelbarrow race.

Those of us left at the tank shake our heads.

'Where'd he get them, then?' asks Maisie. 'Didn't grow them on his plot, I can tell you.'

Maisie keeps a stern eye on her neighbour, Felix, and frequently manages to limit his roguish behaviour by spotting his plans and spoiling them. In fact, Maisie's dedication to limiting Felix's nefarious activities is one of the reasons I still believe she won't hand in her allotment key in November, despite her repeated claim that she will.

But this time Felix has us both nonplussed: it makes no sense at all. Why would Felix be bringing strawberries in to the allotments? Where did he get them and what is he going to do with them?

The person at the front of the line moves off, and we all take a step forward.

'That's going to cause trouble, I bet you,' Maisie says with satisfaction, but she gets no takers; we all know Felix too well to bet against him being in trouble, sooner or later.

16 June

To the plot in my nominal lunch break, to check the spuds. What I want to do is sit in the sunshine and admire the plot, but that's not an option. Instead I have 45 minutes to water, weed and harvest and then, with any luck, eat a sandwich as I walk back home and sit down for another joyous afternoon of writing – this time about the history and uses of galvanised iron.

As I trudge along the path to The Voodoo Plot, I try not to look right or left for fear of seeing any of our more established neighbours taking their ease in a deck chair, whilst enjoying their immaculate, well-tended allotments. One of the problems with taking over a plot that's been neglected is that you have crops appearing where you didn't plant them and don't want them, and volunteer potatoes are the absolute pits in that respect. It's also the pits that I can't take this lovely afternoon off, so that I could work on the plot at my leisure, but my deadline is immovable and I'm grumpy as a result.

A volunteer (or rogue) potato grows from one that's been left in the ground at harvest time. If you miss a single tiny tuber when you dig up your crop, you can bet it will quietly lurk until spring and then sprout madly overnight, right in the middle of something fragile that doesn't like to be disturbed. That's not the worst of it, though. A tuber that's been in the ground over the winter may be harbouring wireworms or blight, or – if you're really unlucky – both.

So we're being vigilant about our potatoes. Our former plot was riddled with wireworm as the people who rented it before us liked to plant potatoes, but appear to have been less interested in harvesting them. The first year we put spuds in, we got exactly five whole potatoes back from the 48 that we planted – every other potato had been travelled through by wireworms, which renders the tuber inedible. The only way to deal with wireworms is to rotate crops and keep turning the soil to disturb the larvae.

Blight overwinters in tubers too, as a microscopic spore called mycelium which can carry off your entire potato crop and your tomatoes and aubergines as well. Early signs are brownish patches on yellowing leaves: if not removed, those leaves tend to curl up and white bloom develops on the underside as the foliage dies away. This is a fungal bloom and the spores from it fall into the soil and cause damp dark spots on the potatoes and reddish-brown stains (like rust or blood) to run through the flesh. You can pick or cut off the damaged leaves and dispose of them away from the plot, but the blight may have already travelled underground. If you don't catch it immediately, or if it travels from a neighbour's plot, you can lose your crop.

As a result, I have become a potato examiner. I check for the first sign of blight and if I find it, cut the haulm (the proper name for the potato growth that happens above ground – stems, leaves, flowers and all) down to the ground and put it in a bin bag to take away from the site. I pick up all and any debris from it and when we do harvest spuds, I do not allow any diseased leaf or stem, or rotten or damaged potato into our compost heap. It's just not worth losing an entire crop.

Today we have a potato that's died back, and I lift the plant immediately to see what the problem is. Fortunately it looks like one of the many site foxes has had a dig in the soil around the potato and snapped the main stem of the haulm, rather than some vile disease or pest launching a career of potato destruction. It's annoying, particularly as there are only a couple of immature potatoes on the root system, but there's no risk of spreading an infestation, so I just compost the whole thing.

I see Felix in the distance but I don't have time to stop and chat, which is frustrating because for once he is sauntering around as if he has time to spare, and I'm dying to know what's going on with him and whether he's secretly taken over an untenanted allotment and started an intensive strawberry-raising business. Instead I trudge back to my car, grumbling under my breath about the unfairness of life and why allotment-holders shouldn't have to work for a living in summer.

Dealing with pests

Ants – pour 3 litres of boiling water directly onto the nest; cinnamon/flour/talcum powder will deter ants when laid in a thick line around fragile plants (this only works until it rains or a strong breeze removes the deterrent); efficiency is promised by commercial ant killers (don't ask, it's a horrible death, apparently).

Aphids – prevention is better than cure and pinching out the tops of young plants is the best way to deter blackfly. Watch out for those nasty ants, mentioned above, as they 'farm' aphids for their honeydew and when you see ants running up and down a plant they probably have a colony of aphids at the top. Just as we keep cows for milk, ants milk the aphids of the sugary honeydew they secrete as a result of sucking nitrogen from our crops. In addition, the ants protect the aphids from their natural predators, like ladybird larvae, so while ants and aphids have a mutual admiration society, it spells destruction to the allotment harvest! If aphids do overrun your allotment, spray affected plants twice weekly with around a teaspoon of biodegradable washing-up liquid in 2 litres of water. Ladybirds love aphids, but once they've eaten a goodly few of them, the population drops too low and the ladybirds, or more accurately their larvae, wander off to find more aphids, and the little plant molesters begin to multiply again. It's difficult to balance intervention and natural means: if you use the soapy spray, it is likely to deter (which means damage) ladybird larvae as much as aphids. Our answer is to try to spot the larvae and move them, but not everybody has the time or inclination to do that.

Cabbage white butterflies – check the undersides of brassica leaves daily and squash any eggs you see there: remove visible caterpillars, wearing gloves just in case they are not cabbage whites but some species with toxic bristles or the ones that shoot goo from orifices, and dispose of them (I find a boot heel delivers instantaneous execution); encourage insect-eating birds by offering winter bird food.

Red spider mite – the only effective control I know for greenhouse spider mite is *Phytoseiulus persimilis*, an even tinier mite that feeds on the eggs and larvae of the red spider mite – can be used April to October in a glasshouse, is not cheap, but really does the job. It's also very temperature dependent, so in a cold spring it might not reproduce at the rate necessary to remove the mites. Keeping greenhouse humidity levels high is a good way of stopping the mites getting to plague proportions so spray the floor, mist your plants and don't store unused pots or trays in the greenhouse as they provide a perfect nesting place.

Slugs and snails – barriers are the least invasive solution – coffee grounds/diatomaceous earth/copper all provide something that gastropods hate to crawl over or die from exposure to; beer traps or milk traps are fun to fill but horrible to empty; toads, centipedes and slowworms all feast on crawlers so encourage these helpful residents by providing habitats they will enjoy. Toads love marshy areas and damp stones to live under, slowworms like open compost heaps and dry stones to live under, and centipedes like any kind of stone to live under. In other words, small heaps of stones, dotted around the allotment, are a real investment in pest control!

Wasps – call your local council and allotment officer if you have a wasp nest. These are not items for amateur removal. Wasps are not a problem unless you annoy them, and sooner or later you *will* do something to annoy them as they have a very short fuse – wasp stings are not fun and a nest contains a lot of aggressive wasps on the alert for threats, so prompt action to deal with wasp removal can save you, or a hapless allotment neighbour, a lot of pain.

Rats and mice – traps, poison or a little dog! Rodents are creatures of habit and they train their offspring to the same habits, so if rodents eat your broad beans or peas when you sow them in open ground, you're going to have to eradicate the population because while there is still one rodent that remembers where to find broad beans or peas, they will turn up at the same time next year and sniff around for their accustomed feast.

Sowing and growing

- Successive sowings of your favourite **salads** should continue every fortnight, but if the season is very hot, allow an extra week between sowings or the plants will all catch up. Rocket will bolt (which means it flowers on thick, bristly, inedible stems rather than producing tender new leaves), radishes get woody and lettuces develop stringy main ribs which are tough to chew through, so having young crops emerging means you can be ruthless about composting the less tender and delicious older harvests.

- **Picking beans** like the **French, wax** and **runners** can be sown outdoors now if you didn't start them earlier under cover.
- **Beetroot** – the striped, golden and other less common beetroot varieties are best sown around now in my experience. Germination of beetroot can be patchy: we like to pre-soak all our beetroot seeds except the very reliable cylindra. Simply tip the requisite amount of seed into a jar and cover it with ambient-temperature water for about an hour before sowing, and sow more than you think you need to as you can always thin the rows.
- **Carrots**
- **Courgettes** can be sown now – with our slug-ridden plot we raise the plants in pots set in trays of sand and only plant them out when they are big enough to survive a slug attack. Even then they get a sand-and-coffee-grounds barrier around them.
- **Fennel** is best started now. It's a crop that bolts at the slightest excuse, and I've found that too-early sowing is the primary cause of bolting.
- Late **peas**
- **Kai-lan broccoli** – which is used primarily for stir fries in the UK – can be sown outdoors and if the slugs let it survive can be eaten 60 days from sowing. It's a cut-and-come-again crop that doesn't bulk up like other broccolis.

Crop care and allotment tasks

Remember to **thin your sowings** so that they don't get congested as this stops them growing well and can cause disease (or pests) to proliferate in tightly packed ranks. You can eat carrot thinnings: the fine wispy roots are delicious in a salad and the fronds should be taken home anyway and disposed of there, as the smell can draw the dreaded carrot fly from many hundreds of metres away.

Sweetcorn will need to be planted out in June, and in most places it requires a certain amount of shelter if it's to succeed. If you live in a very windy area like us, sweetcorn may not appreciate the chilly gales that can still be blowing in June. However, sweetcorn also needs wind to be pollinated, which is why it is planted in a grid or block formation with about 25 centimetres between the plants in all directions, rather than being planted in a long line like potatoes or carrots. We put a fleece screen around the sweetcorn to about 60 centimetres high to keep the breeze away from the base of the plants while they are tender, but allow them to get the necessary wind pollination to produce cobs once they reach full height.

Good pollination is vital, or you get 'blind' cobs, which are the ones that have some nice full kernels and others that have not developed. To improve pollination, you can slide your hand over the top of the corn stalks when they start to develop tiny downward-dangling flowers from top growth: this is the male flower, which carries the pollen that has to fall on the silky tassels that contain the ovary. Corn is only fertile for about ten days so giving nature a helping hand can really increase the pollination rate. The various corns can be annoying in that they also cross-pollinate like mad, particularly when it's windy. This means that if you plant more than one kind of corn, you'll get cross-bred cobs, which may be less sweet than you'd expected. Agriculturalists suggest that you should allow 350 metres from other plantings of corn, to stop cross-pollination. That seems impossible on an allotment site, but once again, I think our low screening helps to keep the right pollen in and the wrong pollen out as much as possible.

June is a great time to be sowing a variety of **manures** that can be dug in around September. If you have poor soil, either **buckwheat** or **alfalfa** will be excellent, and buckwheat has the added advantage of being a magnet for beneficial insects. They are both manures that should be treated as a legume (pea or bean family) in your crop rotation and both are suitable for strip sowing, so if you take out a patch of spring salad or radish that didn't do quite as well as you'd hoped and you think soil depletion might be the problem, simply sow a pinch of green manure seed and then chop it down and dig it under in early autumn.

This is the month to check your **raspberries,** before the rush of summer tasks overwhelms you. Allow six to eight canes per plant and, wearing some really sturdy gloves, pull out any excess. If they won't pull, try digging them out, but don't cut them, it just encourages the cut stem to be even more productive and throw up two canes where there was only one before! It's also the time to hoe around the canes you are keeping, using a light touch to avoid damaging the roots, which can be very near the soil surface. After hoeing to remove weeds, it's a good idea to mulch raspberries. We use wood chippings supplied by our local council, but you might choose grass clippings (let them dry first) or leaf mulch. A mulch for raspberries serves two purposes: it keeps down annual weeds and conserves moisture. Because raspberries have shallow roots they need lots of rain, or regular watering, and a good mulch allows available moisture to be retained, reducing the amount of watering the allotment-holder has to do.

Check your **melons** – if they have five leaves, pinch out the growing tip and transplant them into their final location. From now on, keep only four strong shoots on the plant, as widely spaced as possible, ideally into a cross or X shape. When you plant out, water them well – melons need almost daily watering, and if they are under cover, make sure you can ventilate them fully on sunny days to let pollinators in and out. Pollination is what 'sets' a melon; in other words, it turns a female flower into a fruit and hand pollination is really tricky, apparently, so you need to encourage insects as much as possible – we plant sweet peas behind our cold frame and scabious and flowering alliums on either side, to draw in bees, hoverflies and anything else that might manage to help 'set' melons!

Squashes can be hardened off and then planted out. They are greedy feeders so give them a planting hole filled with well-rotted manure or compost. Sink a big flowerpot filled with stones, or a litre soft drink bottle with the bottom cut off and the cap thrown away, next to the plant – watering the leaves can lead to mildew and rot. They are also bullying growers, so allow more space than you think you need and have a system in mind to support the growth of your chosen squash: **butternuts** do really well given something to clamber up, as do **Turk's turban** and all the pan type varieties. **Pumpkins** are generally too heavy to scramble up anything, and trying to raise massive pumpkins or marrows off the ground too late in the year can cause damage to the stem that feeds them, so have the bricks, blocks, roof tiles or bits of wood that will keep them off the soil to hand, and put them in place when the fruits are about saucer sized.

Keep weeding around **brassicas** but take care not to damage the firm soil around shallow-rooting plants like cabbages. It's better to hand-weed them or cut weeds off at soil level, than to hoe and risk cutting through the root system that is often just below the soil surface.

Brassicas need summer water too, probably a really good volume of water once a week. Using a watering system such as sinking a funnel-style watering device next to each plant can really help in two ways: it draws the roots down to where the water arrives, and it means you don't have to splash water all over the soil surface with a hose or watering can, so there's no moisture for weed seeds to access for germination – therefore, stronger plants and less weeding!

Crops to harvest

- **Asparagus** – in a hot summer you may need to stop cutting spears in mid June if they become really woody, but with any luck you can continue to harvest it until the end of the month. Then leave the bed alone. Let the ferns form, as they store the energy the plants need to crop well next year. Continue to hand-weed or hoe the surface to remove annual weeds (but don't chop down asparagus fronds by mistake).

- **Broad beans** – pods fill fast on broad beans so you need to check them pretty well daily. Once they get to around 15 centimetres in length, and are firm to the touch, they are ready to pick. While many people tell you to twist the bean pod from the stem, I prefer to cut mine with a pair of very sharp scissors close to the stem. Broad bean stems are hollow and can easily be damaged if you pull and tug a pod from the main plant too forcefully. Try to pick beans in dry weather, as damp can encourage the spread of fungus or diseases into the plant where the pod has been removed, which is another reason I prefer a clean cut to a potentially jagged wound from a hearty tug. If you have a bad back and can obtain a cheap skateboard, they are a brilliant device to help you harvest from a long line of broad beans. Simply sit on the skateboard and scoot along the rows with your basket or trug on your lap! Works for peas too...

- If you planted **onions** from sets in the winter, they are probably ready to harvest now. Overwintered onions fill the gap before autumn-ready onions and they are generally mild and juicy, but they don't store particularly well, and will start to flower if there have been temperature fluctuations in spring that trick them into thinking they've been through a short winter, so check them whenever you go to the plot and if they are starting to flower, or the foliage is bending over, lift them by sliding a fork underneath each individual onion so that it simply pops out of the soil. If you're not ready to take an onion or two home on the day you're at the plot, but the bud is forming on a tall stalk above the onion, simply snip that bud off. The onion will not grow any further once it's tried to flower, so I tie a little bit of wool around the flower stem to remind me that I should take that particular onion home soon, as it isn't going to get any bigger! My preference is to lift bulbs that have started to flower on the day I see the bud, if possible, as there is some suggestion in recent agricultural research that a chemical reaction occurs in the flowering onion that can trigger others to flower so your whole crop can be affected if flowering bulbs are left in the ground. If you 'finger' your onions now, they will get substantially bigger in the next seven to ten days, at which point you harvest them. To finger onions, just loosen the soil around the roots – the old guard do this by poking around the roots of their onions with their fingers, but I tend to use a round-ended bamboo cane. It seems that the loosening of the soil, especially in clay areas, encourages the onion roots to take up moisture and to swell the bulb so that it becomes fatter. After a week or so we notice an increase in onion girth and that's when we harvest them. As they aren't storing onions, the extra juiciness doesn't evaporate away over the long months of storage, and they are wonderful for eating raw in salads as they have extra succulence and crispness.

- The early **peas** may be ready now – ours usually are as we start them off in January and grow them under fleece just to get the earliest possible crop. If your pea pods are filling but not yet filled and your plants are tall enough, you can pinch out the pea tendrils and eat them: it encourages pod fill, which means more peas and bigger peas per pod, and gives you a delicious foretaste of the treats to come. Harvest peas from the bottom of the plant up to encourage it to continue production. Because peas are a cool season crop, you will probably have either a good pea harvest (cool damp spring) or a good strawberry harvest (hot spring) but very rarely both.

- **Potatoes** may be ready now. In the sunny south we often start harvesting in the last week of May, while more northern allotments could have to wait until late June to lift first earlies, but either way the new potatoes will have a delicious flavour and the quicker you get them from plot to pot the better they will taste.

- **Rhubarb** will still be available, especially if you've got a crown planted in partial or dappled shade. It may become rather stringy, especially in a hot June, but it can still be used to make excellent jelly, or finely diced into this month's recipe. Make sure you cut down any flowering spikes that appear: they look impressive but weaken the plant and shorten its productive life, so as soon as they start to shoot up, cut them out of the plant. Watch out for secondary flower stalks that won't grow so high and can hide under big rhubarb leaves: if the plant gets to set seed from flower spikes it will probably give up producing edible stalks for several years.

- Early **strawberries** will be ready and high season ones just starting to ripen in June. It's worth having several varieties of strawberry plant to increase the length of the season, but don't assume you have to buy them. We wander round our allotment site, spotting strawberries that are ready earlier or later than ours, and then offer to swap potted runners of our own plants with runners from those plants. It means everybody gains fruit and nobody pays a penny.

Recipe of the month:

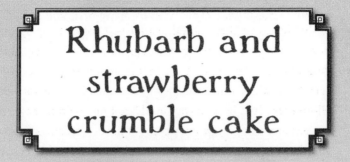

Rhubarb and strawberry crumble cake

This is a fairly traditional crumble cake but most recipes online are confusing and not in the right order: for example, if you make the cake batter before you prepare the rhubarb and the crumble mix, the batter starts to go flat. Given that it doesn't rise much at best, making the various layers in the right order can massively improve the quality of the finished cake. After a couple of years of experimentation, I've adjusted the recipe to work better, be quite a bit healthier and to combine the last of the rhubarb when it's all huge and khaki-coloured and not very appealing looking, with the first of the strawberries for an extra kick of sweetness.

This is a favourite dish in my family, even with the ones who don't usually like rhubarb, and I make it quite often when the rhubarb has become a glut crop on the allotment.

Cake
80 g butter or margarine
80 g caster sugar
2 eggs
80 g self-raising flour

Fruit

400 g rhubarb
75 g strawberries (home-grown and fresh are best; you can use frozen but the texture isn't really as nice)
1 tbsp brown sugar

Crumble

75 g margarine or butter at room temperature
40 g plain flour
50 g muesli or rolled oats and chopped nuts
25 g caster sugar

Preheat oven to 190°C/gas mark 5. Grease a 22-cm round cake tin.

Slice the rhubarb into short pieces and toss in the brown sugar. Leave to blend while you make the cake and topping. Halve any really big strawberries but keep the others whole and set aside.

For the topping

Cut the butter or margarine into the flour with a blunt knife to create small cubes, then stir with a fork to combine, before adding the muesli and sugar and mixing with the fork. It will look lumpy. It should. Don't panic.

For the cake

Cream the butter (or margarine) with the sugar, beat in the eggs, and then fold in the flour – I use half wholemeal and half white but most recipes make it with all white.

To assemble

Stir the strawberries into the rhubarb, then tip the whole lot into the cake tin and spread the cake mix over the top – it will be look quite thin and flat but don't worry, it works out fine. Sprinkle the crumble over the whole thing.

Bake for about 25 minutes and check the muesli isn't browning too much – if it is you can turn the oven down to 160°C and cook for a further 30 minutes or put tinfoil over the top, turn the oven down to 180°C and cook for a further 20 minutes.

It's difficult to check if this cake is done as the rhubarb always makes the batter seem a bit soft when you stick a skewer in. Leave in the tin for ten minutes before loosening the sides and cutting it. It's really more a pudding than a cake but either way it's delicious, especially when served with Greek yoghurt or thick cream.

July

1 July

Compact and Bijou, formerly our local lovebirds, have given up arguing, or so their neighbour Fred tells us as we queue up in the shop to buy tomato feed, having once again failed to calculate just how greedy our tomatoes will be. Having seen their last argument, I find this amazing. Then again, if I hadn't seen that argument I wouldn't have believed they could argue at all, so the whole site is completely astonished that two tubby, chuckling, happy-go-lucky guys have descended so swiftly into a relationship war.

'Oh yes,' he says, with grim satisfaction, 'they aren't talking now.'

'Why?' OH and I ask together. Since we moved to The Voodoo Plot we rarely see Compact and Bijou and we miss news of their forays into allotment life. They are like a Gilbert and Sullivan operetta: frothy, fun and totally enjoyable – perhaps they aren't the best growers on the site, but they have often been the best company. The fact that I saw them brawling with each other on their plot just a few weeks ago shocked me so much I haven't mentioned it to anybody. I suppose by keeping quiet about it, I'm able to pretend it didn't happen. With Maisie threatening to abandon the plot, and our previously happiest allotment couple engaged in relationship sniping, it sometimes feels as if the whole site is collapsing into anarchy.

'On grounds of the fences,' says Fred and then refuses to say more.

As a result of this mysterious pronouncement we take the long way back to The Voodoo Plot and are rewarded by the sight of Compact and Bijou's allotment, neatly divided by not one but two fences, starting at the bottom of their plot and running in parallel on either side of the paving that serves as access to their shed. Each fence has its own gate, opening onto the main path. One fence is a white-painted picket while the other is a pale blue trellis affair. The white fence has sweet peas planted along it, while the blue has a metronomically regular spacing of lobelia, nigella and cornflowers. Both fences follow the paving right up to the shed, ending either side of the door. OH and I look at each other.

'I wonder how often they have to pass each other on the path?' I say.

'I wonder if they've put a fence through the shed?' he says.

We go back to our own allotment, feeling a sense of harmony: we may bicker a lot, and sometimes fall out over horticultural issues, but we've never felt the need to partition our growing space.

17 July

Celia calls me and we spend the day tracking down the tiny seed pods of a peculiarly densely foliaged, silver-leaved alpine that she has been raising on a scree mound on her allotment. It takes two pairs of hands to manage the magnifying glass, tweezers, scissors and brown paper packets necessary to harvest the miniscule seeds. We've agreed, without words, that we won't talk about any of the things that might cause trouble between us: she won't mention her membership of any horticultural associations that I consider to be snobby, elitist and socially inept, and I won't obsess aloud about whether I can find some way to keep Maisie, my wonderful allotment mentor and owner of nicest shed I've ever seen, on our site after her declaration that she's leaving in November. As a result, we have a lovely time: Celia tells me all about the alpine, which is the most boring and insignificant plant I have ever seen, but which is also verging on extinction and only kept alive through the dedication of people (for which read fanatics) like Celia, and I pretend to be interested. I tell her all about the quest my favourite garden writer, Beverley Nicholls, undertook to recreate a Dutch Master, flower by flower, and although she's probably heard the story dozens of times, she pretends to be interested in turn.

When we have something horticultural to absorb us we are a great team and I go home with an aching back and a sense of achievement: 43 seeds have been saved and will be distributed to other growers to raise and save in their turn, so that the almost unknown plant can be kept alive. It's like conserving pandas… only much less cute.

28 July

Every year OH and I make a list of the allotment-holders (often described as 'feeble' or 'not serious' by more dedicated growers) who are taking a summer break, and offer to schedule picking and preserving trips to their plots. The deal is that we get to keep three-quarters of whatever we harvest, and they get back a quarter of their crops in whatever form we've managed to preserve them.

It's a habit we got into during the long years we spent on the allotment waiting list and we still enjoy visiting other people's plots and seeing what they grow and how they grow it.

For some of our elderly allotment neighbours we also, with some trepidation, prune plum trees in July. Well, I say it's for them – it's for us, too, as we have no plum trees and I like being given buckets of Victorias and damsons as payment for my arboricultural activities. To many people it seems counterproductive to prune a plum in the very season in which it's going to fruit, but the best time to cut an overgrown plum is in high summer. It was for this reason and no other that I was up an extremely large and leafy plum tree on an allotment that overlooks Felix's shed, which is how I came to see him trudging along the path with two huge plastic tubs, one in each hand, full of apricots.

I am truly mystified: (a) there isn't a single apricot tree on our site, and (b) once again Felix is heading *towards* the allotment with his produce, rather than away from it, in direct contravention of the law of horticulture that says you arrive empty-handed and leave with harvested crops.

I try to climb back, and although I am only a couple of feet too high to simply step down, I manage to wedge one foot in a bit of tree I can't get that foot out of, while the other foot descends rapidly to earth, leaving me doing a kind of vertical splits. This is, in truth, my usual method of getting out of a tree. Falling out, sliding out and tumbling out are all systems I have perfected – it's just descending gracefully that still seems to elude me.

Once all of me is at ground level I pause for a few seconds and work out my next step. Obviously Felix is up to something, and obviously it's none of my business.

On the other hand, this could be just what I need to keep Maisie involved in allotment life, so rather than taking my usual route to problem-solving (rushing to Celia's plot over the road and getting her rational brain to pick holes in my excitable thinking) I saunter off and take two left turns, so I end up approaching Maisie's plot, which adjoins Felix's, from the opposite side.

Felix has vanished into his shed and I desperately want to go and peek at what he's doing, but instead I head into the crop maze that is Maisie's summer planting scheme to try to track her down.

I hear her talking to herself in the bean avenue.

'It's no good you hiding,' she's saying. 'I know your game.'

For a moment I think she's already giving Felix a piece of her mind, then I realise she's just scolding a vast runner bean that's trying to skulk out of sight. She snaps it from the vine, gives it a disgusted glance and swiftly pops it open with her thumbnail, taking out the beans which she puts in her pocket. Then, as I watch, she shakes her head, takes the beans out of her pocket and lobs them onto her compost heap. There couldn't be a clearer indication that Maisie is still determined to give up her allotment at the end of the autumn and won't be saving beans to plant next year. My heart lurches as I admit to myself that nothing we've done has changed her mind.

I tell her what I've seen, and she shrugs. 'Never trouble trouble while the dog's sleeping.'

It's such a classic Maisie-ism that I take it entirely in my stride. 'But the dog's not sleeping, it's wandering around with buckets of apricots! Don't you want to know what's going on?'

Maisie shakes her head.

'But he could be getting into all kinds of trouble!' I pause to think about that for a second and amend the statement. 'OK, he's always in trouble. He could be getting other people into all kinds of trouble. Remember the manure?'

Long before I even knew our site existed, Felix had a spate of selling sacks of manure to allotment-holders. He was buying them from a stable lad at a local livery. It worked brilliantly for a while and then demand outstripped supply and the stable lad began to feel the pressure... and ended up sneaking into other people's stable yards with a plastic shovel and bin bag to acquire their manure. He was caught when an elderly and stroppy Shetland pony that was given the run of a yard pinned him in a corner and gave him a good kicking. The story had become legendary.

Maisie shrugs and turns back to her beans. After a few moments I head back to my tree. Perhaps Maisie is just waiting for me to go so that she can cross-examine Felix. I just can't believe she's going to let him extend his career of crime without intervening – it would be as unnatural as the sun rising in the west.

Pruning fruit trees in summer

Silver leaf is a deadly fungal disease which travels as spores from dead and decaying wood into freshly cut tree limbs – it particularly favours plum, cherry and apricot trees, although it will destroy apple orchards too. Because the spores thrive in cold and damp, pruning fruit trees in summer is the best idea, and while a variety of forms of wound treatment used to be recommended, there doesn't seem to be any research-based evidence that they help.

Over the decades of allotment unpopularity, many allotment trees were neglected and often new plot-holders have no idea how to get them back into productivity. It feels like a horrible dilemma for those with old, top-heavy fruit trees, because they either have to prune in summer and hope to avoid silver leaf, or leave well alone and hope that winter wind damage doesn't harm the tree and allow *Chondrostereum purpureum*, the full formal name for silver leaf, to get a hold anyway.

If you decide to work on your tree, aim to prune it so that it has an 'open heart', meaning that air and light can circulate around the inner branches. Begin by removing any crossing branches using well-sharpened secateurs and cutting above and sloping away from a bud. Cut back any long limbs that don't have leaves or flowers – reduce their length by about two-thirds. If there are large bare outer limbs, you may need to get expert advice, as anything that's too big for secateurs may need a pruning saw. On these outer limbs, make sure you rub away buds developing on the lower trunk to stop the tree become even more congested.

The pleasures and perils of perennial fruit

Harvesting currants and gooseberries is part of the joy of summer, but it's also the easy bit.

Growing **currants** usually starts with planting bare-rooted bushes in winter. Really soak the roots in a bucket for 24 hours before planting, and set the bushes in the ground about 5 centimetres deeper than the mark on the stem that shows where they were planted in the ground at the nursery. There are many varieties of currant, and bushes last around a decade, so the key thing to note is that the further north you are, the more important terms like 'hardy' and 'frost resistant' become. Check if your chosen currant is self-fertile: most are, but some need another currant to pollinate them. If your currant isn't self-fertile, make sure the two varieties you choose will flower at the same time.

From April, or even earlier in a bad year when there is little spring greenery around, you'll probably need to net the bushes to stop birds taking the fruit. Once avians get used to the presence of fruit, many currant bushes never actually get to set any berries, as birds, particularly pigeons, will peck off the soft green leaf growth in spring, which usually stops the fruit appearing at all. Make sure your netting extends to the ground, as birds are very good at sneaking underneath, but then they fly into the netting and panic and generally die of shock… but not before they've eaten all the currants! If you can, make sure your netting is not small enough to trap the long bony toes of birds that might try to perch on it – every year there are a few horror stories of birds trapping their feet in fine mesh netting and ripping their toes off as they fly away: this can also happen with the plastic mesh in which fat balls are purchased.

A well-manured, well-netted currant bush will produce up to 5 kilograms of fruit annually, and all currants freeze very well, although the vitamin C value of the frozen fruit does fall off the longer it's frozen.

Currants need to be pruned to remain productive – and understanding how they fruit will help you prune effectively. First-year stems do not produce fruit. Second- and third-year stems are highly productive, fourth-year stems have massively reduced productivity. This means that after three years you need to remove formerly productive branches completely. If you're a nervous pruner, here's a foolproof guide to successful currant pruning:

- Year One – plant bushes and leave them to grow freely.
- Year Two – in late winter (or early spring in the very far north) before new growth begins to show, select six healthy stems that are evenly placed around the currant bush and tie a little bit of coloured wool to them, or dab them with a bit of emulsion paint. These are your '1' stems which should fruit in the summer ahead. All other stems should be pruned away close to the point where they join the main plant.

- Year Three – all the new branches that appear in the spring and summer are '2' branches. In late winter or early spring (as above), remove every other one of the '1' branches: this keeps the heart of the plant open and allows air to circulate. Now select six of the '2' branches that are strong and nicely spaced both around the plant and around the remaining '1' branches. Mark them with different wool or different coloured paint. Remove all the other '2' stems close to the main plant. You should be left with around three '1' branches and around six '2' branches – all of which will fruit beautifully in the following summer. Lots of new growth will appear, and that should be considered '3'.

- Year Four – once again, in late winter or early spring, get your pruners out! Remove all the '1' branches, half the '2' branches, and mark half a dozen '3' branches, nicely spaced, around the plant, to be retained. This year, both '2' and '3' will fruit, and new growth should be considered as '1' so you can start the process all over again…

Gooseberries are even easier. They also need to be netted against birds but pruning is simpler by far.

Prune in winter – select a thick pair of gloves and find a stool or similar seat to perch on. At best working with gooseberries is time-consuming and at worst it's painful and daunting, so ensuring you don't become overtired or develop backache is important to get the job done effectively. You need to keep the centre of the bush open to air and sun to get a good crop, and it just incidentally means you can harvest the fruit without becoming an involuntary blood donor! Crossing, tangled branches are difficult to pick from and produce less fruit. Take out any dead or diseased stems first, then step back and look for any branches that cross in the centre of the bush – cut them out too.

Take every branch that is downward-angled back to an upright side-shoot and thin any overcrowded branches ruthlessly. Finally, shorten any old branches back to a young shoot and shorten any new branches by half their length. You end up with a smaller gooseberry bush that's shaped a bit like a wine glass (ideally, anyway – mine usually look like somebody's first attempts on a potter's wheel!) which will be just as productive as a plant twice the size.

Sowing and growing

There's still time to sow:

- **Endive**
- Many forms of oriental leaf vegetable: we like **wong bok, pak choi, tatsoi, mibuna** and **komatsuna,** most of which can be eaten as salad leaves or left a couple of weeks and stir-fried. They are all prone to bolt in hot weather so you need to keep an eye on them and be prepared to have an impromptu stir-fry if they begin to flower!

- **Lettuce** and **rocket**
- **Beetroot**
- Late season (often called potager) **carrots,** although in many parts of the UK they will need to be sown in a raised bed with fleece over the top to keep out the dreaded carrot fly. We like scarlet Nantes for late carrots, although the seed can be difficult to get hold of. Try to find 'heritage' varieties – they are shorter and stubbier than more 'bred' carrots and can therefore be ready in 60 days from planting, while their longer and more slender descendents struggle to get such a fast growth rate and need more watering.
- **Radishes**
- **Turnips** and **swedes**

Crop care and allotment tasks

Remember that however sick you get of **runner beans,** you have to pick all the mature pods when you see them because once they start to dry out, they send a signal to the parent plant that it has completed its task of raising a new generation of beans. This signal switches off flower production so there will be no more beans.

When harvesting **carrots,** do so in the evening and take carrot tops home with you. If you don't, they are like a beacon to carrot fly, sending out an aroma that draws the little flies to your crop, to lay eggs that then hatch and eat into the carrot roots, making the harvest inedible to us.

Watering is going to be a major task in July, with any luck! **Hoeing** the soil actually helps hold water in, counterintuitive as it seems, so breaking up the soil surface regularly is a good idea for water retention as well as for weed removal. We use mulches to keep the soil moist and friable and to protect plant roots from baking in hot sun... if we get any!

If the **strawberry** season is over – which depends on the varieties you are growing – you should remove the straw that's raised the fruits from the ground, trim away any runners (long stems with a rosette of leaves on the end, that may already have rooted in the soil some distance from the parent plant) if you aren't ready to raise new plants from your old ones, and cut off yellowing leaves and immature fruits that won't now ripen, as both can harbour botrytis, the fungus that causes strawberries to develop a hairy grey mould. Birds should be encouraged to peck around in the plants, grabbing insects and snails from under the leaves which would otherwise cause problems for next year's fruit harvest. Most strawberry plants are highly productive for three to five years, and then they become weaker and produce smaller fruit and fewer of them. At this point it's easy to make fresh strawberry plants. Instead of cutting off the runners, pin them to the ground with a pebble or piece of bent garden wire, about 3 centimetres from the little tuft of leaves. If they are barrel- or bed-grown strawberries and there isn't ground for them to root into, just lift them and set the leaves into a small pot of compost with good drainage and weigh the stem down into the pot, alongside the floret of leaves. Water lightly and allow to root. Don't try to establish more than four or five runners from a parent plant. If you are establishing a new crop of strawberries, define where you're going to plant them at the same time you start the runners rooting and dig in manure or compost to provide a rich but well-drained soil.

In the greenhouse, remember to keep removing side-shoots from **tomatoes** and water them every other day at least to stop them drying out, which causes blossom end rot. Tomatoes, **peppers**, **cucumbers** and **chillies** will all respond well to a feed of specialist tomato food or home-made comfrey tea. Keep the greenhouse well ventilated in July or pests and rot will take over and destroy your plants.

Maincrop **potatoes** will also enjoy a liquid feed: comfrey or nettle tea is good, or if you've taken runners and large, healthy but ageing leaves from your strawberries, you can steep them for 14 days in a bucket of water, dilute it by adding two more buckets of water, strain out the strawberry detritus and water that onto your potatoes – they love it!

Where you've lifted first or second early potatoes you can sow a green manure. Mustard is best as a deterrent if you've found eelworms in any of your spuds, but as it's a brassica, take care not to sow it if you have any clubroot on your plot. Field beans are a good alternative to mustard but won't deal with eelworm larvae.

Plant out the last of your **leeks** if they aren't in the ground already.

Start feeding your **lemongrass** with liquid comfrey feed every couple of weeks – it takes around a year for the plant to establish enough for new stalks to grow and it can take two years if the summer is poor, but eventually, each original stalk becomes two or three stalks, topped with up to a metre of grassy growth which is sharp-edged, like pampas grass.

This is the month to plant out overwintering **broccoli** and **calabrese, cabbages, winter cauliflowers** and **kale**, but remember they will all need protection from cabbage white butterflies.

If your **melons** have set fruit that are now between ping-pong-ball and golf-ball sized, it's time to move to a high potash liquid feed every week until the fruit starts to change colour (at which point feeding will make the rind too soft). Keep only three or four fruit per stem/vine or none of them will grow to full size and take the growing tips out of each stem or they will run rampant and not allow the fruit to swell fully. Give more ventilation to melons now, to discourage rot and powdery mildew, and put a roof tile or board under each fruit to prevent damage from the soil. Some people recommend using straw, but we've always found that it encouraged woodlice to move in and although they don't damage fruit, as such, if there is any bruising, cracking or other harm to a melon they will get right in there and exploit it!

Crops to harvest

This is a major month for harvesting. You can expect to be eating:

- The last of the broad beans and the first of the **French beans**.
- **Cabbages, cauliflowers**
- **Celery** and **cucumbers** are both at their best this month.
- **Cherries, gooseberries, raspberries, loganberries** and **tayberries** are all at their best now and **apricots** and **blackberries** should be ready very soon. Depending on the variety you are growing, you may have **white currants** and/or **redcurrants** and, by the end of the month, **blackcurrants**.
- Glut crops in July are **courgettes, lettuce, spring onions, radishes, runner beans, tomatoes** and maincrop **peas**. Also cucumbers: these are a real 'love or hate' food, like **Jerusalem artichokes**. I'm not a great cucumber fan, but OH adores them and we've tried most varieties from crystal apple through to burpless and cornichon. One reason I'm ambivalent about cucumbers is that they seem to have no sense of proportion and insist on trying to take over the world, let alone the plot! You can pinch out the growing stems, but in my experience they just throw out new stems from the centre to replace the stopped growth.
- Leaf crops from **kale** to **lettuce** and **spinach**.
- Summer **onions** should be lifted now, and **garlic** and **shallots** will probably be ready to harvest by mid July.
- First and second early **potatoes** are harvestable this month and as they don't store well, you may wish to plan menus to make the most of their delicious fresh-from-the-soil flavour.
- Root vegetables like carrots and **beetroot**.

Recipe of the month:

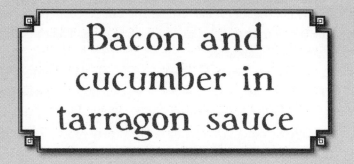

Bacon and cucumber in tarragon sauce

Approximately two large cucumbers (or one huge one, or three smaller ones, as you wish; the recipe seems to work whatever the amount), peeled and sliced into 5-cm batons

Pinch of salt

30 g butter

20 g plain flour

6 slices of bacon, cut into approximately 5-cm strips

1 tsp olive oil

150 ml vegetable stock

75 ml double cream

2 tbsp fresh French tarragon

2 sprigs fresh dill for garnish

Tip the prepared cucumber into a colander and sprinkle with a little salt. Weigh down with a bowl on top and some tins or heavy vegetables in that bowl, and leave to drain for an hour – this releases excess moisture and makes the cucumber easier to work with. Then tip onto kitchen paper or a clean old tea towel to dry the surface of the flesh.

Melt the butter in a large frying pan and sauté the cucumber sticks until pale brown at the edges, usually around five to seven minutes. Set aside.

In the same pan, add oil and fry the bacon gently until cooked then sprinkle in the flour and stir around to absorb the bacon juices. Drizzle half the vegetable stock into the pan, a little at a time, to convert the fried ingredients into a smooth sauce and allow to simmer, stirring constantly, for three or four minutes until well combined and thickened. Then add the remaining stock to the pan, increase the heat and continue to stir until the liquid reduces by about half. Pour in the cream and stir for around two minutes and then tip the cucumbers back into the mixture with the tarragon, add seasoning to taste, spoon into bowls and top with dill garnish. Serve with rice.

August

13 August

Felix has hardly been seen for the past fortnight – in fact, I was beginning to wonder if he had done the thing no serious allotment-holder would contemplate (taking a summer holiday), but that idea seems so unlikely that it doesn't last long. Anyway, I don't have much time to consider what he's doing – I'm too busy organising the buffet for Celia's first meeting of The Exotics. The task of cooking something from each of the continents was an interesting challenge and I can see how the results might impress a bunch of socially inept growers as it will allow them to pontificate and try to find little-known geographical facts with which to impress each other. However, Antarctica presented me with more problems than I'd imagined, and I have a vivid imagination.

The fact is, no Antarctic seaweed has ever been turned into a widely eaten dish, and Celia was adamant that nori and carrageen were not acceptable substitutes for a true Antarctic recipe. We were stymied, until I thought about sea urchins. There are definitely sea urchins in the Antarctic and they can be eaten – and not even the most fanatical Exotic could tell the provenance of a spiky sea creature. Celia reluctantly agreed that it was an acceptable compromise to use urchins on a seaweed crouton. Sea urchin on grilled dulse bread is going to be delicious – I know this for a fact, because uni, the gonads of a sea urchin, are a Japanese delicacy which I've eaten many times, know how to cook and can even buy, frozen, from our local Japanese supermarket. Today is the day that Celia's plans for horticultural domination are to be tested.

Meantime I am watering allotments for people who do have the nerve to go away in summer, and enduring a kind of low-level contempt from more hardcore allotment-holders who think such frivolous behaviour on the part of their neighbours should be rewarded with drought, weed infestations and possibly even squatters. During my regular trudges from plot to water tank and back again, I am being barracked by a couple of the old guard who do not approve of pandering to people who dare to abandon their plots for a fortnight. I'm not paying them much attention, as my mind is focused on how to keep Maisie with us. I've tried a variety of approaches, including getting another allotment association to invite her to be a judge of their annual competition and sending little Lola down to ask Maisie to help her design a square-foot garden for her nursery school. It hadn't worked out as I planned.

We've all known Lola since birth: she's a real allotment baby, although now she's at pre-school we don't see as much of her as we used to, so I was convinced that being involved in Lola's 'baby-garden' project would be an incentive for Maisie to give her plot one more year. I was resolute about not hanging around to see what happened, so after Rachel (Lola's mother) and I had watched her walk down to Maisie's plot, I got on with helping Rachel prune her raspberry canes. Less than five minutes later, Lola reappeared and toddled her way back up to us.

'What did Maisie say?' Rachel asked casually.

Lola frowned. 'She says she is leaving soon, and so I need to ask somebody who can help me choose what to plant all through the year, not just now.'

'Oh, OK, we'll do that then.' Rachel sounded cheery but the look she gave me over the top of Lola's head was tragic, and I suspect my own expression was equally forlorn. We both learned our horticultural skills from Maisie, and can't really imagine the site without her.

I didn't have time to stop and console Lola, who is anyway a pragmatic little creature like most horticulturalists, because in-between lugging water around, harvesting tomatoes and cucumbers and wondering where Felix is, I am mentally totting up the timetable for cooking, packing up, delivering and unpacking tonight's buffet and coming to the terrifying conclusion that I should have left the allotments half an hour ago.

14 August

My poor timing was the least of the difficulties experienced during Celia's attempt to impress The Exotics with her suitability to be their Chairperson. Even before the buffet, the evening was doomed, apparently.

Having dropped off the dishes of food, along with simple colour-coded instructions on what to reheat and what to keep chilled, I was not an observer of the disaster because I am not, and never will be, the kind of horticulturalist that The Exotics would invite to join them – the privilege of spectator was Stefan's and it was he who enlightened me the following morning as I sat with Hattie Jacques on my lap, to listen to the disastrous tale. 'Hattie' is one of Celia's cats: she names them after comedians. One of the reasons Celia approves of me (on balance, and after careful consideration, she does approve of me, although there are many reasons she disapproves too) is that I name my dogs after fictional detectives.

The disaster began with a very opinionated male orchid grower interrogating Celia on her progress with the *Tillandsias*, and degenerated from that point.

After the orchid expert had tutted his way through a critique of Celia's cultivation techniques, the meeting opened with a point of order that took nearly an hour to settle. The agenda itself required a further two and a half hours, so by the time they were ready for supper, the dishes that had been keeping warm in a low oven were little more than clinker and ashes.

Celia is, as I may have said before, no cook. Unperturbed by the scorched and smoky offerings, she banged hot dishes and cold alike onto the table and went into the kitchen to restore herself with a double Martini, leaving The Exotics to serve themselves.

The result was that a committed vegan ate three helpings of the sea-urchin bruschetta before lifting the serving plate to find the charred sticky note adhering to the underside on which I had printed NOT FOR PEOPLE WITH SHELLFISH ALLERGIES, at which point she promptly had a fit.

'Not an anaphylactic one,' Stefan reassures me. 'Just a common or garden hissy fit.'

Celia's lack of care with the *Tillandsias*, compounded by 'undermining a lifetime's commitment to cruelty-free living', led to a mass walkout of the committee.

Celia, left to deal with the debris, told Stefan that 'cruelty-free' was only true if you ignored the lifetime's unpleasantness one human being inflicted on others in the pursuit of faddy eating, and went to bed with the Martini pitcher, where she still was.

I gathered up my clinker-encrusted plates and dishes and left quietly. Best to let humorous cats and hungover horticulturalists lie.

15 August

I am hiding out at the allotments. Celia rang early this morning and suggested that we get together to discuss ways to reassert her authority over The Exotics. Fortunately I was in the garden and she left her message on the answering machine, giving me the opportunity to escape. I know she knows where to find me, so instead of lurking on The Voodoo Plot I have come down to Maisie's, where I feel moral support is likely to be available. Maisie and Celia have mutual respect, which is a way of saying neither has the upper hand, as yet.

Now I'm here though, sadness descends as I walk past the raised beds that Maisie is clearing as the crops finish. Her broad beans, peas and early potatoes have all been harvested and each bed has been dug over and a green manure planted. Now she's digging in the green manure so the new plot-holder will have perfectly conditioned soil in which to begin their horticultural career.

When she sees me, Maisie hands me a scythe and instructs me to cut down the red clover to within an inch of the ground so she can fork it into the soil. There's no such thing as a bystander on Maisie's plot.

I work slowly, because a squadron of bees is trying to extract pollen from the clover as I'm trying to cut it and while I have no fear of bee-stings, I don't want to whack a slow-moving, heavily laden bee with my scythe.

She lifts her chin and points to Felix's plot behind her own. 'He's been in there all day,' she says. 'Sulking.'

'Why sulking?' I negotiate my blade between two semi-somnolent insects and hack some foliage to the ground.

Maisie snorts. 'I don't have time for his capers.'

It's a bit like being in an Ealing comedy, right down to the vocabulary, and I half expect Felix to appear with a spiv moustache and a suitcase and offer to sell us some black market seeds that 'fell off the back of a barrow'.

When Maisie decides it's time to put the kettle on, I nip next door while the tea brews and knock on Felix's shed. After a couple of seconds the door opens. Felix looks haggard and doesn't manage to raise a smile even though I hold up the pork pie I brought with me as bait.

'Maisie's making a brew,' I say. 'If you've got tomatoes, we can have pie and tomato salad…'

Felix shakes his head. 'I can't face her today.'

That's not unusual. When Felix has been more than usually rascally he often finds dealing with Maisie difficult, but this time he's even struggling to meet my eyes.

'What's up?' I ask.

He shrugs and slides back into his shed like an eel hiding in a crevice on a wildlife programme and I follow him into the gloom to prise the story out of him.

'You know I've been selling soft fruit,' he says.

I nod.

'Well, it's run out. And so have I.'

I wait patiently, knowing that Felix is about as discreet as a funny ringtone. He simply can't keep quiet.

'I found this monastery,' he says. 'Well, nunnery really, although they call themselves a monastery.'

'Was it lost?' I ask, but my irony is itself lost on him.

'They have tons of stuff. And I do mean tons. Rods of strawberries, orchards of fruit, glasshouses full of vines, jungles of raspberries, acres of hot-beds... most of it going to waste. So I said I could... find a use for it. They were glad about that.'

I note the emphasis on 'that' and keep my head down, cutting the pie with his excellently sharp asparagus knife.

'They *were* glad about it, really glad. Until the Daughters turned up.'

'Daughters?' I have a vision of a Chaucerian nunnery, with bawdy nuns indulging their base passions in the strawberry beds and raising a horde of godless babies.

'Daughters of Righteousness. Women who aren't nuns but like being with nuns.' Felix is gloomy. 'Women who visit the nuns every quarter and do stuff.'

My mind is still with Chaucer, so 'doing stuff' sounds very racy.

'Stuff?' I enquire.

'Bottling strawberries,' he groans. 'Making apricot butter. Stuff like that.'

'Oh. And...?'

'And the Daughters seemed to think I bilked the Sisters out of their harvest.'

'Ah.'

'And you'd think they'd be a bit more religious, wouldn't you? But one of them got really nasty.'

'Nasty?'

'Sort of... litigious. She said she was a lawyer and the Sisters would sue me. Sue me! I was giving them a cut.'

'Let me get this straight. You sold their fruit and gave them a cut. How much?'

'Well, there was a value-added component. I had to pick the fruit. The Sisters helped a bit… but they're elderly, I did most of the work. Then I had to box it all up and take it to the market. It was quite demanding.'

My mind is reeling at the picture of Felix getting a bunch of elderly nuns to harvest their own soft fruit, so he could flog it in the street. 'How much, exactly, was their cut?'

'Well, about ten per cent.'

'About?'

'Well, ten per cent minus my expenses, of course.'

'Oh, of course.'

Felix chews moodily on his pie. 'They're picketing my flat until I stump up the rest of the money I made.'

The vision shifts – now I am imagining nuns with placards pacing in circles outside Felix's block of flats. 'The nuns?'

'The Daughters. They sit outside in a car. They shout at me.'

I am inclined to agree that this sounds rather unspiritual but on the other hand, the determination of the Daughters is quite impressive – they seem to have got the measure of Felix very quickly.

'They sound more like Daughters of Retribution. So that's why you're hiding out here?'

He nods.

'Well, don't let the committee find out you're sleeping in your shed.'

He gives me a guilty, supplicating grin and I realise, with a little jolt, that for the first time in my life I have the edge over Felix. I exploit it immediately.

'I won't tell the committee you're kipping on the plot if you think of a way to keep Maisie on her allotment,' I say.

Felix looks stunned. 'Why would I want to do that? She's the bane of my life.'

I lean forward menacingly. 'No, she's not. The Daughters are. You have a choice between a rock and a hard place. I suggest you consider Maisie your rock.'

He nods slowly. 'I'll think of something.'

'Good. Be quick.' I leave him the pie as sustenance and make a note to take him a flask of tea before I leave for the day. We're both hiding out, after all.

Water conservation for summer crops

Using water efficiently isn't just about beating hosepipe bans. Plants grow better when watered effectively and the grower has to spend less time on a boring and, if there is a hosepipe ban, back-breaking task and can devote more energy to the fun and productive parts of growing food.

The answer is mulching. To mulch is to cover exposed soil with a layer of material. It has four benefits:

- It minimises water evaporation.
- It regulates temperature by reducing sun exposure.
- It reduces weed seed germination.
- It limits soil compaction, which damages soil fertility (dry baked soil forms a crust that is hard to work and low in nutrients for plants).

You can mulch with lots of different materials: straw, bark chippings, hay, newspaper, grass clippings, compost… anything biodegradable will usually work. Just about the only thing you can't mulch is seeds and seedlings as the mulch will usually scorch the tender immature leaves and soft stems of seedlings and kill them off. Mulching is a vital step to reducing the amount of watering you have to do, so it's worth planning ahead and researching how you can mulch each of the crops that you intend to grow – most allotment books give some idea of which mulches will work for which plants, but local knowledge is the best source: ask established growers for their tips and keep a record of your successes and failures so you can improve on your productivity year on year.

Picking the right time – it's best to water early in the morning or in the evening. Evaporation can remove 40 per cent of the water that is placed on or around plants when they are in the sun, and scorching – which happens when droplets of water act like mini magnifying glasses – can damage leaves. Morning watering is ideal, as high moisture levels overnight can encourage problems like blight to spread, but evening watering is fine, as long as it's not indiscriminate spraying around with a hosepipe.

Less is more – check the soil. Plants only need water if the soil at around 10 centimetres deep is dry. If they have established root systems, they can extract water from damp soil at that level and soil moisture increases with soil depth so the deeper the roots go, the better the plant is able to take care of water needs. Seedlings will need daily watering until they are established, but after that you can water every other day, as long as you give them a really good soak, which allows the surface water to soak down without evaporating. Adequate watering encourages seedlings to develop strong, deep roots to seek out water, giving you a better crop.

Water the roots – efficient watering means getting water to the roots, not the soil. The fad for perforated hoses seems to be waning at long last, at least on allotments where such pipes either clog up, get cut through by garden tools or are unusable in drought conditions, which is good, because there are several ways to water more efficiently. Use funnel or bottle watering as described in June's allotment tasks. Plant rows of seeds in slight troughs, to ensure the water you give them runs towards the roots, not away from them.

Be water rich – harvest and store as much rainwater as you can. Water butts on sheds and greenhouses can keep you water wealthy for months. Corrugated plastic sheets at a slight angle over our compost bins run into a gutter that runs into a dip tank from which we fill watering cans. The rainwater we gather is used to water the plants and the nutrients in the compost aren't washed away into the soil when it does rain heavily. Make sure water butts and barrels have lids to stop midges, or worse, mosquitos, breeding. Tanks should have lids too, but more importantly, give them a mesh or net covering so that creatures like frogs, toads, mice and even hedgehogs don't get in and find themselves unable to get out.

Summer holidays

If you're going away, don't forget your crops. Some sites now ask you to ensure an allotment neighbour waters, weeds and harvests your crops, while others leave it to you to decide how to manage your plot during your absence. To come home to a happy allotment, ensure you:

- Water plants thoroughly before you leave.
- Deepen mulches.
- Harvest everything that is ready and store or preserve it at home.
- Remove immature fruit and flowers from plants that you don't want to produce crops while you are away: snip off flowers from courgettes and squashes, pinch out the side shoots of tomatoes and scour your beans to be sure you've taken away every single maturing pod that could halt flower production.
- Offer the produce from your plot to somebody who is willing to weed, water and harvest while you are away – and if yours is a gated allotment, make sure that neighbouring plot holders know to whom you've lent your key, to avoid unpleasantness!

Sowing and growing

Sowing is slowing down now, although there are winter crops to be readied. There's still time to sow late season carrots and baby turnips.

- **Radishes** can go in the ground but in very hot weather they may become woody before you can harvest them – it's a gamble worth taking for the pennies that it costs to buy radish seed!
- **Endive, chard** and **oriental salads** can all still be planted and **perpetual spinach,** if you like it, can be sown in August too. In the last week of August we sow ordinary spinach in long troughs in the shade: it will serve as cut-and-come-again leaves until November, when we take it into the greenhouse and get another month of slow growth out of it before it becomes totally dormant around Christmas.
- **Kohlrabi** will still come good if sown in early August, so it's worth planting them where you've taken out a spring crop such as early peas or broad beans.
- Winter crops to be getting under way in seed beds are **spring cabbages** and **red cabbage.**
- **Savoy cabbages, cauliflower** and **winter kale** should be ready to plant out now, even in the most northerly or exposed areas. As they will live through much of the winter, preparation done now saves you a lot of time in the months when weather is bad. Give each plant a water bottle, funnel or other root-watering system so that you can irrigate them but not the surrounding soil. They all need firm treading down when

you put them in the ground, as they have to get through the winter without being damaged by gales, etc. Many will need staking – do it now, not when they start to sway in the winter wind! Remember your caulis will need protection against cabbage whites and your cabbages and kale may be at the mercy of slugs, especially if there are a couple of days of heavy summer rain.

- Consider planting Christmas Day **potatoes** – there's no guarantee you'll get a Christmas harvest, but some time in December you should get wonderful fresh new spuds. The best time to plant is the second two weeks of August and we always start ours in containers, at first outside and then, before the first risk of frost, moved into a cold greenhouse. We use tubers from the Carlingford potatoes that we harvest in the spring. Simply put some nice-sized tubers to one side in a cool airy place and give them a fortnightly spray with seaweed solution or comfrey tea to help the shoots develop. We fill containers with compost and set three potatoes in each container. It's important to avoid blight, which can still strike potatoes through to October, so we usually put some horticultural fleece over the top of the containers when they are outside. The easiest way we have found to do this is to turn a wire basket upside down in the top of the container, and lay the fleece on top of that to stop it touching the foliage. Remember to water the spuds and move them out of frost range in the autumn and you should be rewarded with delicious potatoes around Christmas time.

Crop care and allotment tasks

Feed your **Brussels sprouts** now with a seaweed or blood-and-bone feed and ensure they are well firmed down or wind rock may loosen the roots, causing all your sprouts to become open-hearted flowers: pretty to look at but not so nice to eat!

Keep **hoeing** open areas of soil as you remove crops: this stops the soil compacting and prevents late germinating weeds getting a hold – it's easier to hoe them in now than to weed out in a few weeks' time.

Check your winter **squashes**: fruit will benefit from being lifted from the soil on bricks or old roof tiles and it's a good idea to cut away leaves that may be shading the developing fruit as the better the air circulation, the more likely the fruit is to avoid getting blossom end rot. Calcium deficiency is one cause of blossom end rot in squashes, and applying calcium nitrate (a water-soluble form of calcium that the plants can access through the soil) is the short-term solution. Poor air circulation intensifies the problem as the weak cell walls in the fruit collapse and mould spores proliferate in the damp warmth created by the sheltering leaves and spread into the microscopic cracks in the expanding squash or pumpkin. The long-term solution is to improve your soil quality – it saves all that other work! If you have the space, it's good to allow your winter squashes to clamber up canes and other supports – we provide ours with sturdy twiggy branches to cling to, and this both increases air circulation and makes it more difficult for slugs and snails to find the newly formed baby squashes which they love to munch on when the outer wall of the squash is still tender and easy for them to chew through.

As summer **raspberry** canes stop producing fruit, cut each cane down so that the newly emerging canes, which will fruit next year, have maximum exposure to light and air from the very beginning.

rosemary

Mid to late August is a good time to cut down the top growth of maincrop **potatoes**. This is said to make the skins less prone to damage when you lift them, which may or may not be true; I can't say I've really noticed a massive difference but it's definitely true that if you cut the top growth down level with the soil now, blight is much less likely to get into the plant and destroy your hard-earned harvest.

sage

Cut back **herbs**, propagating any that you want to reproduce. At this time of year you can take semi-ripe cuttings of **bay**, **rosemary** and **sage**, and divide clumps of **mint**, **lemon balm**, **lovage** and **chives** to produce vigorous new growth. Shear back **thyme**, **oregano** and **marjoram** or they will become leggy and woody. You can still be planting pots of **basil** as seeds will germinate and produce vigorous growth this month.

thyme

basil

In August, give the **asparagus** bed a good hand-weed, a feed (we use granulated all-purpose feed)

mint

and then a mulch: our preferred mulch is grass clippings from the lawn, which feed the soil and keep it friable so that the surface does not compact in the heat.

Check the **strawberry** runners you pinned down in June; sometime between mid August and early September they need to be separated from the parent plant. To tell if they are ready, examine the leaves – if you see large bright new growth, they have rooted. To be sure, lift a runner gently with a hand fork and see if it has nice strong roots. If so, cut all the runners from the parent plant with sharp secateurs, close to the baby plant, and then make sure you cut the rest of the runner, which is like an umbilical, from the parent plant too. Transplant new strawberries immediately into their final home, or pot them into a size larger pot in good rich compost and put them in a warm but not too sunny position. Remember that if you're keeping them through the winter in relatively small pots, they will need much more protection from frost and wind than their parents did. It's best not to plant strawberries back into the same place their parents grew in, as soil-based diseases (called pathogens) can proliferate and kill off young plants. If you're planting in a new strawberry bed, space them 30 centimetres apart with 40 centimetres between rows for ease of harvesting: strawberry plants spread out a lot, and I've never yet met anybody who said they'd planted their strawberries too far apart, but I've met dozens who complained that they'd planted them too close together and now found it difficult to harvest fruit from one plant without damaging the fruit on another nearby.

Crops to harvest

- **Aubergines** should be ready by mid to late August and are harvestable when they develop a glossy skin.
- **Beetroot** should be at their best in August, so try some new recipes: we like beetroot and cheese pie, beetroot hummus and of course, beetroot soup!
- **Summer cabbage**
- **Calabrese**
- **Carrots**
- If you grew **celery**, this is the time to harvest it – past the end of August the stems will start to hollow and become woody.
- **Cauliflowers**
- **Cherries**
- **Cucumbers** will start to dry and yellow if you don't harvest them in good time. As they grow so fast, a daily check is recommended.
- **Globe artichokes**
- **Lemongrass** may be ready now. Wearing gloves, pull and twist one of the newly formed outer stems from the main plant. Usually they leave the parent very easily and then need to be trimmed back to useable length. The parent will continue to grow and divide as long as it doesn't get frost damaged. You need the gloves because the grassy top of lemongrass is capable of slicing through skin, like pampas grass does.
- **Marrows** and **courgettes** are at their best now too and will soon approach glut proportions, as will **French** and **runner beans** and **tomatoes**. Marrow chutney is a good solution to a marrow glut, and home-made piccalilli is a fun way to use up many August glut crops.

- **Melons** raised in hot beds are likely to be ready by the end of the month.
- Storing **onions** should definitely be coming out now if they're not already lifted and drying. Harvest them on a sunny day and let them dry in the sun for as long as possible before removing dry soil from roots, and then netting them or plaiting the necks and hanging them up to continue drying.
- **Sweet peppers** and **chillies** will be changing colour if there is enough sun, and that's a sign they are ready to eat.
- Early **pumpkins** like **patty pan** and some **butternut squashes** may be ready to eat now.
- **Raspberries** and **blueberries** are in season along with **apples, blackberries**, the late **redcurrants** and **blackcurrants, pears** and **plums**.
- **Sweetcorn** should be ready by the end of the month. The first sign of readiness is that the translucent white silk tassels become beige or deep brown: then you can peel back a little of the covering (called the husk) and push your thumbnail into one of the kernels. If it is ripe, a milky substance will ooze out. If the corn is not quite ready, the juice will be watery rather than milky. If you've been unlucky enough to let the cob get overripe, a sort of grey, porridgy mush will emerge instead!

Recipe of the month:

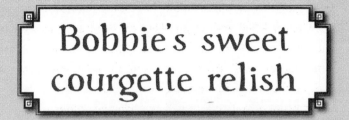

Bobbie's sweet courgette relish

500 g courgettes, finely chopped
1 large onion, finely chopped
250 g apples, finely chopped
250 g raisins soaked in herbal teabag-infused water overnight
(I particularly like raspberry and vanilla teabags)
220 ml cider vinegar
175 g granulated sugar
2 tsp wholegrain mustard
1 tsp galangal
½ tsp dried chilli, flaked or crushed – we use royal black chillies
that we grow ourselves
1 tsp coriander seeds crushed with ½ tsp black pepper
2 tsp cornflour

Put the courgettes and onions in a large, heavy-based saucepan and pour in the cider vinegar as you stir to mix thoroughly.

Add the sugar, mustard, galangal, chilli, cornflour and coriander/ pepper mix. Stir over a gentle heat until the sugar has dissolved and then bring to the boil.

Reduce heat, add raisins and apple and cook for around 40 minutes to an hour, until the mixture has thickened a little – it will be more runny than chutney but it firms up in the jar.

Spoon into hot sterilised jars and seal. Keeps for six months.

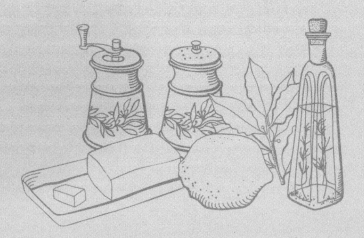

AUTUMN

September

6 September

My birthday. I receive an excellent present – a cast-iron chimenea. Not only is a chimenea a great way to keep warm in winter, it's also a brilliant way of disposing of small amounts of rubbish such as perennial weeds. We're lucky enough to be on a site that permits enclosed fires throughout the year, and I am excited by the idea of having a stove on which to warm my hands in the bitter winter months and which allows me to destroy dandelion roots in the process!

We take my new pot-bellied delight to the plot and stand it where I think it looks best while we go and shake the borlotti beans to rattle out any dry beans from their pods and pick tomatoes to make chutney.

After a couple of hours of intense harvesting we decide it's time for tea and head back to the shed, only to find that my lovely gift has listed to one side in the soft soil and has to be dug out by OH while I slide planks under the clawed feet to try to distribute the weight more evenly. Obviously we haven't thought this through properly.

8 September

We are levelling the chimenea for about the eighth time since my birthday when Felix appears, looking more confident than he has for some time. 'I think I know what to do,' he says.

I wait expectantly.

'The problem is that Maisie needs more time to spend with Mr Maisie, right?'

I nod.

'So, I know somebody who can help convert her plot to hydroponics. No weeding, no watering, lots of crops. She'll get the time she needs, and still be here when she wants. I've arranged for Brenda to come along tomorrow and give her a demo.'

This seems a bit abrupt to me, but it's true we don't have any time to waste. Maisie's plot looks increasingly bare and her shed is emptying steadily as she takes home or gives away her tools.

9 September

It's unfortunate that Celia happens to be around when Brenda arrives.

Hydroponics has never appeared on my horticultural horizon, although the term 'vat' in a somewhat sinister 'mad scientist' sense does cross my mind whenever I hear hydroponics said aloud: I had always put this reaction down to reading way too much science fiction as a teenager (and to watching horror films where monsters always seemed to be floating in vats of fluid) until I saw Celia's reaction to Brenda.

Maisie, sitting in her favourite deck chair and sipping ginger beer, appears remarkably relaxed about proceedings and it didn't take me long to discover why – Felix had led her to believe Brenda was here as his girlfriend, not as the solution to the problem of keeping Maisie herself on her plot. Given that Maisie views Felix as something between a poorly housetrained dog and a delinquent child, she's always happy to see somebody else taking on supervisory duties in his life.

Celia, though, becomes white-lipped and white-knuckled. She drags me behind Felix's shed where, shin deep in stinging nettles, she berates me. 'How can you let the prophets of mediocrity set foot in a repository of horticultural richness?'

I'm not sure where to begin, and decide that a redirection of her question is the best route. 'I didn't,' I say with spineless promptness. 'This is Felix's doing.'

Celia drags me back to the front of the plot, which I am starting to think of as the 'arena' and Maisie blandly nods at her whilst handing me a bunch of dock leaves she's pulled from the path. I bend to rub my smarting nettle stings, noting that Celia seems immune to pain and that Maisie is definitely enjoying our drama more than the demonstration. My heart is sinking again.

Brenda sets up a bench on which she props a length of drainpipe with holes cut in the top. Then, with funnels and duct tape, she attaches hosepipes to each end, tips gravel into the drainpipe and then tapes a gallon container to each of the hosepipes: one container is full of clear liquid, the other empty. There's also a car battery, a solar panel and a bunch of leads and plugs. Mad scientist indeed! It looks like a miniature distillery.

She starts an explanation but Celia hardly allows her to get two words out. 'Isn't it true that hydroponic food cannot be given organic status?'

Brenda's answer is about soil certification and the fact that no soil means you can't get certification, so it's a technical issue.

Maisie isn't an organic grower anyway. Like most of us she's a 'largely organic grower' which means she'll take the least damaging route available, whilst reserving the right to go nuclear on a particularly troublesome pest or weed. She leans over to me and says, 'She's quite a bit older than him, but I think that's all to the good, don't you?'

I nod, cravenly aware that Celia thinks Felix invited Brenda here all by himself and that Maisie thinks Brenda is Felix's new love, and sooner or later this level of misinformation *has* to be my fault, because it always is.

'Isn't it also true that the major crop harvested on home hydroponic systems in the USA is marijuana?' Celia counters.

Brenda launches into an explanation of the laws governing medical marijuana production in the United States.

'Ah, that's why Felix is so enamoured,' Maisie whispers. 'I did wonder. Still, at least where love is blind it can't smell the rotten apple in the barrel of fish.'

I don't even bother to untangle this particular set of Maisie-isms. Instead I watch as Brenda and Celia, toe to toe, start a slanging match in which terms like 'empty traditionalism' and 'environmental thriftlessness' are being thrown around. Felix steps in-between them with, 'Ladies, please...' and they round on him immediately, Brenda wagging her finger while Celia digs him in the ribs with an elbow, both talking at once.

With one mind, Maisie and I stand up quietly, step backwards over Felix's side fence and continue our reverse progress until we are hard up against Maisie's bean canes, at which point we duck, dive, and continue to weave backwards into the plot until we can creep into her shed, pull the door closed and the blind down, and collapse, sighing, into her easy chairs.

'She'll keep him busy for a while,' Maisie opines. 'But faint-heart never won a beauty contest and I think Felix's eyes will soon start to water.'

'Wander,' I correct, half-heartedly, sadly aware that the hydroponic honeymoon is over before it started, and we are no closer to persuading Maisie to stay than we were in April.

23 September

Celia is busy. I'm not sure what she's doing, as she appears to be hiding from me. This is a weird situation, as usually it's me hiding from her, but she's definitely being evasive and even the offer of cake hasn't brought her out of her seclusion. Stefan tells me not to worry so I go back to making tomato chutney, but my mind is still uneasy.

25 September

I am hunting for more lemongrass. I could buy it from the supermarket but I am temperamentally opposed to doing this. The problem is that the tomato glut and the pepper glut have wiped out my supply and we've rather got habituated to the tangy depth that it gives to chutney. I've used up all the lemongrass from the greenhouse, except the two stems that I've replanted to provide a harvest for next year. I really don't want to buy lemongrass – it would feel like buying broad beans, something I haven't done since 1994! So I trudge up to the top of the site, on a humid afternoon, to ask Jeremy if I can have some of his. Actually, it's been a while since I've seen Jeremy who is one of our 'freelance' allotment-holders. Like me, he works from home and tends to visit the plot when he's not got paying work, so his presence is a bit unpredictable.

Highly unpredictable, I realise, as I reach his plot. The grass path is more of an extremely narrow meadow than a green swathe between crops, and there aren't any crops to speak of. The broad bean plants are still in place, looking like the vegetable version of Giacometti's skeletal figures, and bindweed has grown up around them, strangling the long-deceased plants. There's also the unmistakable smell of a fox having made some part of this plot his or her own – it's a scent, or rather a stink, that would have driven Rebus into a frenzy by now if I'd brought him with me so I'm rather glad I came on this quest unaccompanied by my faithful terrier.

It's starting to feel like a Sleeping Beauty plot, as they are called at one South London site on which I used to be a co-worker.

Sleeping Beauty plots are ones that were originally beautiful but which become overgrown and neglected as their tenant sleepwalks his or her way through the seasons, somehow failing to register that the plan to 'get to the plot next weekend' has been postponed for weeks, then months, then years...

Sleeping Beauties normally begin their descent into vegetable narcolepsy in November, once the big harvest is over and the weather turns nasty. There may be a partial awakening the following March or April, when the Easter holidays bring a reminder that summer is on the way and that last year the plot-holder was planting potatoes or sowing peas during the holidays, but that rousing from semi-somnolence rarely survives the first trip to the plot for six months. Just the sight of the weeds is enough to send most fairytale plot-holders back to sleep, let alone the disgruntled expressions (and maybe comments) from allotment neighbours who are unhappy about six months of weed seeds blowing over their plots. The Voodoo Plot was a classic Sleeping Beauty when we took it on – it had been neglected for over a decade and many people had concluded it had been designated a wildlife reserve by the council!

Jeremy's plot looks bad. I fear the Sleeping Beauty syndrome might have got hold of him even earlier in the year than usual and I can tell there's no point checking in his greenhouse to see if he's got lemongrass – there are things in there that may once have been tomatoes or peppers or aubergines but what I can see through the white-painted glass are just collapsing desiccated shapes tethered to canes. He has no winter crops in the ground: no Brussels sprouts, no cabbages, no purple sprouting broccoli. This plot is not just dying, it's effectively dead.

I pull out my phone and scroll to Jeremy's number, ready to suggest that he and his girlfriend, and OH and I get together at the weekend, bring a barbecue, and blitz this plot back into shape. Then I stop. I can hear OH's exasperated voice in my head asking me how many times we've done this? A quick mental catalogue of the past few years reveals at least six attempts to help floundering plot-holders get back on track and none of them have succeeded. One of the reasons I teach plot management skills is to try to help people get to grips with the year round bit of having an allotment, and the classes I teach are the result of decades of watching plot-holders try and fail and try and fail...

Jeremy has my number – if he wanted help to get his plot back into productivity, he could have called me. He's called often enough before to discuss when to plant or what to plant or to brag about his harvest – I can't force him to be a good plot-holder, and if he loses his plot, hopefully it will go to somebody who has an all-year-round commitment to growing their own food. I'll miss him, because he was enthusiastic and fun to spend time with, but fair-weather allotmenteers aren't pleasant to have as neighbours and while it's a shame to lose his company, the plot-holders on either side of him deserve somebody who doesn't make their lives more difficult.

I trudge back down and prepare to humble myself to Felix, the only other lemongrass-growing allotment-holder I know, but to my great delight he isn't on his plot and I carefully lift four stalks of lemongrass from his greenhouse, taking the entire leafy metre of top-growth to stick in a vase as the scent is very pleasant on a hot day, and leave an IOU written on his white-painted window glass with a licked finger. Felix is a rogue and a rascal but I've known him a long time and the absolute trust of long-time plot-holders pertains here: he knows he'll get a jar of chutney and next time he's short of something, from compost to cauliflowers, he can wander up to The Voodoo Plot and help himself, secure in the knowledge that fair allotment trade is no robbery.

How to preserve glut crops and your good temper simultaneously

Overplanting is the main cause of gluts, obviously! So don't grow more than you need. There's always a temptation to plant out another courgette seedling or another half-dozen runner beans, but seriously – can you eat courgettes and runner beans every day from July to October? If not, don't overplant!

Prioritise harvesting of crops in prime condition and ruthlessly dispose of glut vegetables that are less than perfect before you leave the plot. Once they're in the compost bin you WILL forget about them but if you bring them home you can't help but spend time trying to cut out the bad bits or save the good bits and you'll still be picking over vegetables or shelling beans or cooking chutney at midnight – and the next day you'll have to do it all again.

Trade growing with preserving – you may have a neighbour or family member who is willing to make jams and pickles with the produce you provide, saving you a long hot job once you get home from the plot.

Plant cooperatively – we never grow runner beans: on our plot many people are willing to trade their surplus runner beans for our excess sweetcorn or spinach, so we use the trade system to keep our summer gluts manageable.

Sowing and growing

Very few crops grown in September will make much growth through the winter but there are some plants that will make a crop between September and December that is invaluable for adding variety to a winter diet.

- **Chard**, sown now, will grow slowly but it's frost resistant and will produce cut-and-come-again leaves through the winter.
- **Coriander, chives** and **chervil** can all be sown for the kitchen windowsill.
- **Endive** can be sown now, and is harvestable until December or even January if kept under a cloche.
- **White Lisbon onions** can also be sown until around the end of September – they are a great 'spring' onion to eat through to December in stir-fries.
- **Tender-stem broccoli, rapini** or **kai-lan** are all varieties of brassica that can be sown in September for a harvest in around 40 days. Don't leave them longer as they soon become tough and woody.

Crop care and allotment tasks

Plant **green manures** to be dug in around Christmas time.

Trim back **perennial herbs** like marjoram which get woody if left to their own devices.

Check your **asparagus** bed. If any of the fronds, which are probably yellowing by now, are forming red berries, they are female plants. Female asparagus produces fewer spears and most modern varieties of asparagus are all male – when a rogue female spear appears, dig it out gently or it will seed and compete with the male plants, gradually weakening the production of large spears.

Divide **mint, tarragon, sage** and **parsley**, cutting away any woody and unproductive areas, and replant (we lift our French tarragon, divide it, and put half in a pot in an unheated greenhouse, the other half back in the ground under a cloche, to ensure at least one plant makes it through the winter).

Planting out

- **Spring cabbages** can be planted in their final positions now.
- **Overwintering** (also called **Japanese**) **onions**, which are sold as sets, can be sown for an early harvest to keep you going before your maincrop onions are ready. Make sure the soil you plant them into is friable (if necessary add sand to break up clay soils) and scrape a little dip to pop them into. Don't

press them in with your hand – if they hit a stone they will be damaged and probably rot – and don't plant them too deep. They pretty well sit on the surface. You may need to cover them to stop birds pulling them out. Nothing much appears to happen until spring but all winter, below ground level, they are creating strong root systems so the bulbs can rocket away when the better weather arrives.

- **Melons** should be ripening now. You can tell if they are ready to pick by the fragrance which only appears when the flesh is ripe. Don't rely on the folk advice that the skin will begin to crack near the stem – it doesn't necessarily happen in wet summers or for all varieties so your melons might rot while you wait for a sign that isn't going to appear! Lift a melon that smells ripe and twist gently; if it starts to separate from the main stem, it's definitely ready.

Crops to harvest

- The big **apple** season starts now! Cooking apples can be picked when windfalls start, but eating apples can (and should) be picked a little under-ripe and allowed to finish their maturation off the tree. It's better to plan to clean-pick an apple tree over three or four visits, rather than trying to do it in one day, as in a mammoth picking session you end up tired and clumsy and then you knock ripe fruit to the ground as you reach for apples that turn out to be unripe.

Pick on a dry day as damp fruit rots almost before you get it home. A small basket or large solid-bottomed bag is good for the picking process – and I've never found anything better than a good laundry basket for actually putting the picked apples into. Where possible get a gang of friends to help you so that some can pick fruit while others sort it.

A stepladder is handy, and we have a pick tin – a large metal tin with a V cut out of one side fastened to a long stick. Pad the bottom of the tin with a bit of old cloth. To use a pick tin, push the tin up under the fruit, so that the stem falls into the V, and then wiggle the tin to get the sharp edge of the V to cut the stalk. It takes a little practice but I much prefer it to standing on a wobbly ladder trying for a fruit that's almost out of reach! Hand-picked apples and pears should be set in the palm of the hand and pushed upwards towards the tree as you twist the stem – if ripe the fruit comes away from the branch with the stalk intact. Anything you have to tug at probably isn't ripe and may shake all the riper fruit to the ground where it will get bruised on impact. If you are picking unripe fruit to finish off at home, cut it from the stalk by the spur (the part of the plant it is growing from) with good sharp secateurs.

Don't tip or pour picked fruit from one container to another – if you do you will bruise it and any trapped wasps will come screaming out of the fruit avalanche and probably sting you! Instead transfer each apple or pear by hand, turning them over to check for damage and laying them out, barely touching, in a large airy container.

We separate each layer with old towels. When we get home we check them again before storing them in a cool room in shallow cardboard boxes. Good keepers will last until January if well laid out.

- **Aubergines** may be ready now – if we get any aubergines at all, and we rarely do, we get them in September!
- **Runner beans** and **French beans** will still be going strong.
- The first of the **drying beans (borlotti, Cherokee Trail of Tears, soldier,** etc.) should be readying now – if the pods start to shrivel and turn brown, cut them carefully from the plant and put them somewhere dry and airy to continue the process. Don't pull them from the plant because you can damage the roots by tugging on the bean stems and that stops the plant filling out the remaining bean pods.
- The last of the **beetroot** should be ready – cylinder beetroot can be cooked and frozen for three months, but globe beetroot, in my experience, is better eaten fresh.
- **Blackberries,** both cultivated and wild, are abundant: they can be wiped, open frozen and tipped into freezer bags to process later in the year.
- **Summer cabbage** and **all-year-round cauliflowers** are ready now. Watch cauliflowers carefully, checking the dense white heads for signs of flowering, which manifests as the florets yellowing and expanding outwards into tiny blossoms – eat them immediately if they start to flower.
- **Red cabbage** should be perfect now. Cut the heads once they are solid and remember that heavy rain can make any mature cabbage crack open or split from its stalk. If you cut the head while managing to leave a couple of the outer leaves on the stem, and then score a small cross on the cut surface

of the stem, you'll usually get a few baby cabbages growing at the interstices of the stem and the remaining leaves – they will be about twice the size of large Brussels sprouts and are wonderful steamed whole in a stainless steel pan (don't use aluminium, it turns red cabbage grey) and served with a sprinkling of parmesan and toasted sesame seeds.

- **Carrots** are ready now.
- Greenhouse **chillies** should be ripening now but may need a couple more weeks to reach full flavour.
- **Courgettes, cucumbers** and **marrows** will probably be glutting madly.
- **Globe artichokes** and **cardoons**
- All the **summer herbs** continue – also, **lemongrass** is ready now.
- **Kale**
- **Kohlrabi**
- Early **leeks** may be ready if the weather has been quite rainy.
- Later **lettuces** – often frisée-style lettuces do better after July than hearting lettuces.
- **Melons** in a cold frame should be about ready to eat in a reasonable summer – they won't be supermarket sized, so it's best to think of them as at best two-person melons and at worst, single serving ones!
- Storing **onions** should be ready to come up now – see if the foliage is bending over at the neck, which is the key sign of readiness.
- **Pears, peaches** and **plums**
- **Peppers** will be changing colour now – it's worth checking that they aren't touching each other, as this can cause rot. Take out one of a pair of touching peppers and eat it green.

- Harvesting maincrop **potatoes** is probably in full swing in many parts of the country if you avoided blight. Choose a dry day to dig and fork out your potatoes carefully, or you will spear them and then be annoyed because there is some law of physics, like the one that says toast must land butter side down when dropped, which says you will always stab the fork through the biggest, finest, most perfectly shaped potato on each plant.

  When you have dug them up, let the spuds rest on the soil surface for at least three hours to give the skins a chance to toughen up. Rub or brush the dried earth from your potatoes and store them. Don't wash potatoes, unless you really have to, as it's almost impossible to get them dry again and damp spuds soon rot. Storage systems vary: sand trays, hessian sacks, all kinds of specialist gubbins that you can buy made of canvas with drawstrings and I don't know what else. The basic rules of storage are simple: ensure spuds are dry, undamaged and put somewhere cool, dry and dark. We keep ours in a single layer in cardboard boxes under the stairs!

  If your spuds are at all dirty, consider popping some slug pellets in your storage system. Little tiny slugs can lurk under clods of earth and merrily munch through your potato stock, and slug pellets can't harm wildlife if they aren't out in the open.

- **Raspberries** are likely to be productive now, particularly varieties with 'autumn' in their name.

- **Spinach**

- Early **squashes** like **patty pan** will be a good size to eat, big orange **pumpkins** and other keeping squashes should be curing but not yet ready to harvest.

- **Strawberries** may still be productive for you, depending on where you are in the country.
- **Sweetcorn**
- **Tomatoes,** both indoor and outdoor, should be at their peak.
- The first baby **turnips** will be ready to eat in September.

Recipe of the month:

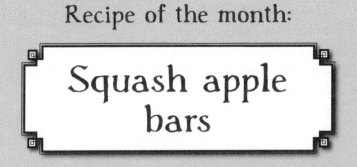

Squash apple bars

You can't make these with courgette or other soft-skinned cucurbits but you can make them with any firm squash and the recipe works around the amount of squash you have, so you can scale it to suit yourself. I have used both cured and uncured squashes with equal success. These are popular with our friends who don't eat gluten – I'm often asked to make them for harvest festivals, etc. They taste a little like apple, hence the name.

Firm-fleshed squash or pumpkin – if you have immature butternuts or other squashes that won't grow to full size before harvest, this is a great way to use them up
Nut butter – either peanut or almond butter works best in my opinion
Eggs
Honey or sugar
Baking powder

Cut the flesh from immature squashes, regardless of their variety, and either steam it or cook it gently with very little water until it is tender. Then mash it or puree with a blender and put into a mug or other container until it's about three quarters full. Tip into a bowl. Repeat if you have more squash until you have measured the number of three-quarter containers of squash you've got.

Using the same container, fill it completely with your chosen nut butter, once for each three-quarter container of squash you counted. Tip into bowl.

Add an egg for each full cup of butter.

Add around a third of a container of sugar, or preferably honey, for each full container of butter.

Add a teaspoon of baking soda for each full container of butter.

Beat all the ingredients together.

Tip into a well-greased and base-lined tin or silicone baker. We use a 20-cm square silicone. Bake for 25 minutes at 160 to 170°C/gas mark 3 to 4.

Cut into squares and serve hot with Greek yoghurt or leave to cool and add to lunchboxes. These bars are very dense, very tasty and something that nobody ever seems to eat just one of, so don't expect them to last long.

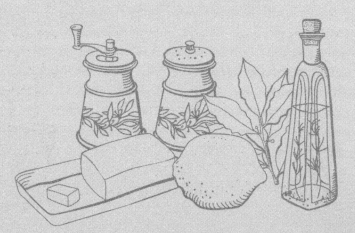

October

12 October

Compact and Bijou have resorted to guerrilla tactics. The committee is trying to empanel me as an adjudicator but I am not playing along. They say it's my technical skills they want: that I have the best digital camera and so can take the necessary pictures of the 'damage'. I respond by offering them the camera to take photographs themselves. Griping ensues. Eventually the committee decide the issue is actually a council one, not an allotment one, and hand it over. 'It' is a pile of documents at least an inch tall as I discover when I agree to photocopy 'it' so that the council and the committee both have a copy of the dispute.

Compact claims that Bijou has been attempting to destroy his Jerusalem artichoke bed by introducing slugs and snails into it 'under cover of darkness' and Bijou says that Compact vandalised his edible border, which ran along the picket fence, by deliberately spraying it with non-organic weedkiller. Both 'deliberately' and 'non-organic' have been printed in bold italics. I can almost hear the outrage in his voice.

The whole situation makes me sad. Disputes between allotment neighbours happen from time to time, although I wouldn't say they were frequent. Maisie and Felix are a perfect example of the kind of bickering, competitive and sometimes acrimonious relationship that can occur when two different growing styles are separated only by a fence.

Disputes between allotment couples often seem less common, but I am coming to suspect that the truth is more complicated: if a couple have an allotment and they fall out, we, their neighbours, probably don't get to hear about it. One or both of them just stops coming to the plot and while we wonder and surmise, we almost never discover what's happened. Every year there will be a few plots that have been left unworked for several months, letters from the council go unanswered, and eventually the committee have no choice but to offer the plot to somebody else.

It's unusual for a couple working the same plot to get into the kind of skulduggery that Compact and Bijou seem to have descended to. It's a fact that they were never amongst our most committed horticulturalists: in living memory they are the only allotment-holders on our site to be given a warning for inappropriate decor. We've had many tenants receive warnings for weeds, trees, rubbish, vermin, failure to cultivate and dangerous crops but *only* Compact and Bijou have ever been told that their statuary was obscene and their 'unusually shaped' crop beds were likely to cause offence to sensitive people.

15 October

Our site seems to have been totally riven with strife this year. Even Rachel and Steve, parents of Lola the allotment baby, were unhappy with each other – because Steve wanted Rachel to give up the job she hated, working as a hotel receptionist, and take Lola out of school and teach her at home. Rachel, while not totally averse to the idea of giving up work, certainly didn't intend to home-school Lola! As she said to me when we bumped into each other at the allotment gate, 'It's all very well Steve suggesting it, but he doesn't understand what happens to women who spend all day with vegetables and small children.'

'You mean the HSM effect?' I said, and she nodded, and on that bleak note of reminder about one of our previous allotment companions, the Home Schooling Mother, and her grim determination to raise her children to be entirely self-sufficient, we parted: Rachel to collect Lola from school and me to ask Celia if she could suggest any way to unite a warring allotment couple.

The only people who were getting along well (apart from me and OH) were Maisie and Felix and that was largely due to the fact that she was 'de-cultivating' her plot and as a result had no opinions to offer Felix on what he was doing and the fact that she was growing fewer and fewer crops each month gave him ever less to comment upon. Given Felix's record with Maisie and Brenda, I definitely wasn't going to ask him for his views on reuniting Compact and Bijou, and Maisie would just tell me it was none of her business as she would be leaving soon, and I was getting fed up with hearing that.

I left the pile of paperwork in the office and wandered off to see who else was around but on a cold weekday morning the site was almost deserted, and after cutting an autumn cabbage to make cabbage pie, I went back home.

17 October

A day spent quince collecting. Quinces are an issue in our house. I have always wanted a quince tree but they are tallish creatures: taller than our allotment site allows. I could keep it pruned to the right height but then it wouldn't produce fruit, and I don't want an ornamental tree, I want a cropping one. It would be entirely possible to have a quince at home, but that would mean cutting down one of the large, ugly apple trees that is already in the garden and replacing it. I would rather have wonderful scented quinces in a few years' time than continue to endure pappy, flavourless apples from an old, overgrown and often diseased tree, but OH doesn't agree, so I'm stuck.

As a result I rely on kind friends to locate quince trees for me and then I beg people for picking rights. I am happy to make quince jelly and membrillo (quince paste) for anybody who supplies me with quinces and I even make quince tree owners their own quince tarte Tatin, which is a real labour of love, but worth it if it lets me procure this particularly fragrant fruit. It is possible to buy quinces, but I have never done so, for two reasons: (a) they are exorbitantly priced

and (b) the shop quinces never seem to have any fragrance which makes me suspect that something about the way they are picked, stored or processed destroys the true value of the fruit which is the incredibly delicacy of the perfume/flavour.

Quinces are also large, hard and obstreperous so quince picking involves wearing gloves and a substantial hat. Many quinces fall early and easily from the tree because of their size and weight, but that can make things more, rather than less, difficult as being hit on the back of the head by a falling quince as you bend to pick up another is quite capable of giving you concussion. By the end of a quince-picking afternoon I am ready to head for a hot bath and something mindless on TV, but it's worth it.

22 October

We have been to the cinema. Celia is sitting on the doorstep when I get home. When she sees me, she walks to the car, opens the passenger door to let OH out and slides in.

'To the allotments,' she says.

'Mine or yours?' I ask faint-heartedly. What I really want to say is 'no' but that's a word I've never really got the hang of around Celia. Actually, I can say it and sometimes I even do say it, but she just ignores me, so for reasons of efficiency I've given up even trying.

'Felix's.'

Well, that wakes me up. I drive slowly, trying to work out how to extricate myself from the position I am likely to find myself in, which is between Celia and Brenda. I am so absorbed in my own thoughts that it takes me a while to realise that Celia is muttering to herself.

'... unrealistic outputs given the inputs... must be some kind of trick... power ratios impossible...'

She sounds like she is channelling dialogue from *Star Trek* (always a possibility – Celia's day job is translating English into a variety of languages, so Klingon doesn't seem beyond her reach) and I fear that the debacle with The Exotics has destroyed her equilibrium. Stefan has, from time to time, hinted at a breakdown from overwork in her twenties.

At the allotments we tiptoe along the path until we reach Felix's plot. I've been hearing a strange whirring sound for some time, but Celia, still muttering under her breath, doesn't seem to have noticed. At the top of the plot we crouch and Celia cups her hands around my ear.

'We're here to find out how Brenda is faking her hydroponics. I've looked up the system and done the calculations and that solar panel can't produce enough power to drive the pump. So let's find out what's going on.'

From tiptoeing we skulk, which is hell on the hamstrings, up Felix's path and the strange sound is louder. Now even Celia is aware of it and gives me a confused look, or at least I assume that's what it is – deciphering facial expressions, even by a full moon, isn't easy. Once we navigate round his brassica cage the noise-maker becomes apparent. It's Brenda, in a pair of old leggings, pedalling away like crazy on a stationary bike. There are allotment rules covering most things, but night-cycling without going anywhere doesn't appear in any that I can recall.

I am ready to stand up and ask what on earth she's doing, but Celia tugs my arm and pulls me away, duck-walking back down the path (oh my hamstrings will hate me tomorrow!) and refuses to speak until we are back at the car.

'That's a bit odd,' I say, then think about all the odd things that usually happen on allotments and realise that it's really not very odd at all. Moon-cycling is probably like moon-cycle planting, only more so.

Celia shakes her head, but not dismissively, in fact the dashboard light reveals that her expression is awed. 'Well, it's dishonest,' she says slowly, 'but it's not unacceptable. In fact, it's a good solution to the problem.'

'You sound impressed,' I say.

'Yes. Yes I am. Dedication. Appropriate solution. Ingenuity.'

'What, exactly, are you talking about?' I am so used to being the village idiot that I don't even sound exasperated any more.

'A solar panel wouldn't store enough electricity to power the pump that circulates the nutrient fluids around that hydroponic set-up, meaning that her plants will die and she can't have that, because she's got to prove me wrong,' Celia says, staring at the allotment gate with her arms folded. 'So Brenda's set up a system where her pedalling generates the power that charges the battery overnight. She's changed the inputs but she's not using an unsustainable power source.'

Dogged perseverance is exactly the kind of characteristic to win Celia's favour, so I'm not surprised that she nods approvingly. 'Devious, disingenuous and physically demanding,' she says. 'Exactly what I would have done myself.'

24 October

I spend the morning turning our compost heaps for the last time this year. I know that my enjoyment of compost turning is peculiar, but I love the process of forking waste material from one bin to another and finding that the bottom of the first bin is full of rich, chocolate brown compost, which can immediately be spread on the soil to enrich it and produce stronger, healthier plants next year.

Ten ways to be a perfect composter

1. Make sure your compost bin is easily accessible, has a lid or cover and is in a sunny or semi-sunny location on bare ground.

2. Compost green and brown in equal proportions: lawn trimmings and tender young weeds, along with the leaves from root crops, count as green. Twigs and woody prunings, along with cardboard, all count as brown. Green breaks down fast but can become smelly (and slimy) while brown breaks down slowly and gives ventilation gaps and bulk to the heap as it decays.

3. Never compost animal products, ash from coal fires, cat litter or dog mess, or nappies. They all attract foxes and rodents and they can all cause putrefaction rather than gradual decay.

4. Hot heaps 'cook' quicker. To make a hot heap you need to cut up all the contents to similar sizes and mix them well together. A hot heap needs a lot of bulk – the bin should be at least two-thirds full and needs to be watered after every

30 centimetres of compost has been added. After a few days it will really heat up! Around a fortnight after making a hot heap, turn it out, trying to get the outside bits into the middle, and adding more water if needed, or more shredded cardboard if the heap is soggy. You can turn it every ten days or so but each time it will cool down as the energy from the composting process is dissipated. When it no longer heats up, leave it to finish composting for a few weeks or months.

5. Cool heaps need less attention. You can make them by adding material whenever you get it, bearing in mind that layers of green and brown should be alternated whenever possible, to get oxygen into the heap. You can ignore it for three months in summer, six if it's made in winter, and then fork it over or turn it over, taking out any usable compost and adding the uncomposted material back into a new heap.

6. Don't add brassicas with clubroot or anything suffering from white rot to the heap. Neither is killed by the composting process. Blight has to have healthy green plants to attack – once the plant is uprooted the blight will die, so you can add blighted potatoes or tomatoes to your heap. Most other diseases like grey mould, mildew and wilt will be killed in a 'hot' heap but possibly not in a cooler one.

7. Be weed aware because some perennial weeds won't be killed even in a hot heap. Avoid adding dock roots, buttercups and celandines (both part of the ranunculus

family), ground elder and bindweed to your compost. You can drown such weeds in a vat of water until they become unrecognisable and then add them to your compost but that tends to get smelly and breed midges, in my experience. We bag them and take them to the tip!

8. Consider activators. These are a blend of nitrogen and protein which help the organisms that break down the material in the heap. Some people use fresh horse or cow manure, some use bone meal or blood, fish and bone, some use comfrey mixed with pelleted fish food(!). We find shredded comfrey and horse manure or chicken pellets work well for us.

9. A comfrey bed can be a valuable addition to your composting skills. While comfrey spreads readily from root cuttings, it rarely sets seed, so grow it in an enclosed bed or container to keep it in check. Cut the stems and leaves, wearing gloves as the leaves contain a skin irritant, and strew them on the compost before you add a layer of other material. They help speed up composting and add nutrients to the heap. Once your patch is established you can cut it four times a year, to about 15 centimetres above the soil level.

10. Be patient – while perfect conditions can produce compost in as little as two months, it can take up to a year.

Sowing and growing

- **Broad beans** can be sown now, but make sure they are overwintering varieties. Until the last couple of years we have always sown our broad beans in the autumn as this definitely reduces blackfly infestation in spring, but in recent years we've lost autumn-sown beans to intense cold and snow in February and March, so we've moved to planting spring-sown varieties in February. We grow them in paper pots under cover in an unheated greenhouse and plant out the entire pot in April. Try both methods and find out which works best for you. If birds pecking out the new seedlings are a problem, cover the bean rows with a layer of horticultural fleece or old net curtains. If rodents, rather than birds, are your bugbear, you can strew holly leaves between the rows to make it difficult for them to walk – it really does discourage both kinds of pest!

- **Cauliflower**

- **Winter radish (mooli)** – are an excellent addition to the winter diet. This long root needs to be sown in soil similar to that required by parsnips: no stones, not too wet and not too rich. The addition of sand is the best way to get the right conditions, or you can grow mooli in a deep container in a sheltered spot, bearing in mind that it can easily reach 30–40 centimetres in length. It's usually ready two to three months after sowing and can be left in the ground or container as long as it's not going to be attacked by frost.

- **Winter (perpetual) spinach** is a tougher creature than the summer varieties but it will still need covering with a cloche or growing under cover to survive well through the winter. It also has a stronger flavour and thicker ribs, so when harvested it needs more picking over and removal of 'stringy bits' than summer spinach.

- Start to sow a **winter density lettuce** like **Arctic king** outside – it'll cope with most weather conditions and give you something green to eat when shop prices go through the roof. Sow every month through the winter – germination will be slow and lower than summer varieties but this way you still get to eat fresh greens right through the year.

Crop care and allotment tasks

Cut away any yellow leaves on your **brassicas** – they serve no purpose to the plant and can act as lurking places for slugs and snails.

On a dry day, carefully dig up the **endive** (Belgian variety) that you want to force through the winter. If you break the main bulb they won't force, so be patient. Once lifted, cut away the leaves and roots (as described in May) and put them somewhere dry and light for five to seven days to cure. Then pot them up in sand, cover them and put them somewhere cold.

Get ruthless with the **strawberries**. Remove all dead leaves and grey rotten strawberries that didn't get harvested when they were ripe. Trim back the plants, removing any runners that you don't want. Remember that each runner that grows takes strength from the parent plant and lessens the fruit harvest for the following year, so only pot up runners when you're ready to start a new strawberry bed.

I like to plant new **raspberry** canes now, so their roots get down before the frost.

Wash down your greenhouse, remove any shading you've left up, and insulate if you're going to be using it to over-winter tender plants.

Turn your **compost**.

Order **asparagus** crowns.

Move **lemongrass** into a heated greenhouse or the porch and keep watering every month or so as it doesn't like to get too cold or too dry. Every third year we trim the grassy top growth to about half a metre and then split the plant into two 25-cm pots so it can divide and multiply further.

Crops to harvest

- **Apples**
- **Beans** – the last vestiges of **runner beans** and **French beans** will be still around now. Even if they are no good for eating, you'll usually find the pods contain beans you can save to sow next year, if this year's beans weren't F1 hybrids. If they were, don't save seed, as it won't necessarily be like the parent plant.
- **Blackberries**
- **Cabbages,** especially the first of the **red cabbage**.
- **Carrots** – lift any left in the ground before frost makes them sweet and bendy!
- **Kale**

- **Kohlrabi**
- **Potatoes** – get your maincrops out now, if they aren't already harvested.
- **Squashes** – if the stems have become dry and woody, it's time to cut and cure them. To do this, with a knife or secateurs cut through the stem, leaving about 4 centimetres attached to the plant. Don't twist or snap it from the plant, as this can cause damage to both plant and fruit. Curing winter squashes allows them to develop an impermeable outer skin that preserves them for months – if they don't cure, the surface remains soft and allows moisture to escape, so the flesh dries out, and can allow mould spores and bacteria to enter, causing decay. Keep cut squashes in a warm, dry, airy place for up to a fortnight, to help them cure. An empty greenhouse is a good solution, or lifted from the ground in a dry area if a greenhouse isn't possible or still contains crops being watered. We often arrange ours on old planks raised on bricks under a 'roof' of clear plastic, and give them a quarter turn every day so that they get an equal exposure on all sides to the sun. Rain and frost both damage curing squashes, so don't let them get damp and cover them if an air frost is likely. After curing, they need to be kept somewhere cool and frost free. Space them out so that the air can circulate and turn them every week to ensure they don't develop soft spots.
- **Swedes**
- **Sweetcorn**
- **Tomatoes**
- **Turnips**

Recipe of the month:

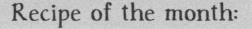

Membrillo

This is quince paste – it's a good thing the Spanish have given us their more exciting name for it, as quince paste cannot begin to describe the absolute deliciousness of this particular confection. Quite what you use it for is up to you: in Spain membrillo is served with Manchego (sheep's milk cheese) which is a perfectly wonderful combination, but our Tudor forbears liked quince paste as a dessert food to have with sweet wine – which is another perfectly wonderful combination. We are very fond of membrillo sliced very thinly and gently warmed in the microwave before being laid over really good vanilla ice cream, but perhaps the most perfectly wonderful combination we've come up with is membrillo with roasted chestnuts and Cheshire cheese. The point is that finding ways to eat this long-neglected preserve has been part of the joy of learning to make it.

There are many recipes for quince paste or membrillo, but almost all of them seem to make very heavy work of matters. For years I used to spend hours peeling quinces – which is a bit like peeling an oak tree – and coring them and so on, until I found a recipe in an old Spanish cookbook, took it to Celia who, although Spanish is not one of her 'fluent' languages, was able to translate it at first sight and confirm the suspicion I'd formed as soon as I saw the illustration. There is no need to peel quinces to make anything! The easy way to work with quinces is to cook them first, cool them, then carve away the skin – it's much quicker and doesn't destroy your hands and temper.

Scrub your quinces with a firm brush in cold water to remove the fuzz. Place them in a big saucepan and cover with water. Bring to the boil, put a lid on the pan, reduce heat to a simmer and cook for around an hour, topping up with more water if necessary.

Cool the quinces – you can plunge them in cold water if you're in a hurry and peel away the skin with a sharp knife, then quarter the fruit (you may still need a cleaver or substantially large knife for this as the cores can remain like solid oak, even after cooking) and cut away the woody core. You'll be left with beige-coloured slices of fruit that look a bit like pears and have a similar granularity.

Put the slices in a blender until they become a thick purée.

Weigh this purée: for membrillo that keeps for six months, you need 250 g sugar for 500 g of fruit. If you want membrillo that keeps a year, you need equal weights of fruit and sugar. You can add a little lemon juice, which helps to clarify the colour, but two ingredients are all you need, really.

Mix sugar and purée in a large, heavy-bottomed pan, and simmer for between 45 minutes and an hour – an alchemical change occurs and the beige paste transmutes to a rich amber or tawny colour, or, if your quinces are particularly good, heads right into the tangerine end of the colour spectrum. The two ingredients combine to become a very thick paste, which needs to be stirred regularly so it doesn't scorch.

Pour this thick, granular jelly into a lightly oiled square baking tin. I now only ever use silicon baking trays for membrillo, as it's far easier to get the paste out of a flexible container. For

Christmas presents I make membrillo in small silicon loaf tins so that it comes out in the shape of ingots and after I've sugared them, I wrap them in cling film so they can be stuffed into the toes of Christmas stockings like gold bars.

Allow the paste to cool completely, at which point it will be a solid, clear, deeply coloured jelly that is firm enough to slice. When it has cooled, turn it out onto greaseproof paper that has been liberally sprinkled with caster sugar and then press more sugar all over the surfaces. The sugar acts as a humectant, keeping the membrillo dry, and once it is well sugared and wrapped in plastic film, it will keep for either six or twelve months, depending on the amount of sugar you used, in the bottom of the fridge. To use, unwrap, slice and rewrap.

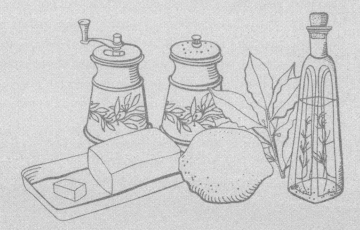

November

2 November

Pyromania – both deliberate in the form of vandalism, and inadvertent in the form of over-enthusiastic or forgetful plot-holders starting fires – is an issue on many allotment sites, so today is the day for going round and checking that nobody has decided to build a huge bonfire on their plot. Bonfires aren't the issue, as such; it's having bonfire parties and fireworks that causes the problems – we're pretty lucky, being a gated site, that only allotment-holders can enter, but there have been a couple of times in the recent past when people held big parties with lots of visitors and fireworks and other people's crops got trampled by rampaging kids or drunk adults, or both. As our site is something of a wildlife preserve, fireworks can be especially damaging to the ecosystem: hedgehogs and foxes, mice, and owls all prefer not to have their evening's activities interrupted by noisy rockets and explosions that light up the sky like the Battle of Britain, and I always wonder if, around this time of year, many of our resident creatures get visits from suburban relatives who are hoping to escape the back-garden pandemonium in the world outside our gates.

It's a tricky issue because people are allowed to have open fires on our site from October until March, which is an increasingly rare privilege. Many sites no longer allow open fires, and quite a few don't even allow incinerators, requiring allotment-holders to compost waste or take uncompostable stuff to the tip. It's also a tricky issue on our site because tempers are running high again. Many allotment-holders are horrified by a proposed rent increase which would more than double the cost of a plot. It's often the case that those who are most aggressive in their complaints have least understanding of the process and take their fury out on our hardworking committee who have no more say in rent increases than we would in the succession of the English crown. As a result, most of the committee are feeling like a bonfire has been lit under *them*, and are sensibly staying out of sight until tempers die down. It's not an easy time to be suggesting to irate plot-holders that bonfires are OK but bonfire parties aren't and that fireworks are definitely out of the question, so I have reluctantly agreed that I can do my bit by making a quick sweep of the allotments near my own and remind any new allotment-holders of the rules.

Fortunately there are no heaps of wood on any of the plots in my block, so I scuttle home, feeling like I've got away with something – although I'm not quite sure what.

5 November

It's back to The Voodoo Plot for me to lift a couple of leeks and cut a cauliflower. To my great pleasure it's foggy, so if there are bonfires ready to be lit tonight, I probably won't be able to see them. I love walking the allotments at this time of year. As the autumn growth dies away, the site develops vistas and views which don't exist in summer when every plot is deep in vegetation growing up, down and sideways, so that the site is like a food

jungle. Most November afternoons, it's possible to see across 20 or 30 plots in a row: bare fences, empty greenhouses, maybe a few rattling dry bean pods on wigwams and frames, brassicas squatting like trolls on the wintry soil, settling in grumpily to survive when everything else dies. Not today, though – and that's when the unplanned magic happens: a vixen, tail down, lollops wearily down a path out of the fog. She's exhausted from raising another generation of unruly offspring, but plump enough to get through a cold winter and probably looking forward to a few long nights without the yipping cubs demanding food. She crosses in front of me, barely glancing in my direction, and her total contempt of my presence is typical – this is her domain, and I'm just an occasional interloper.

On The Voodoo Plot, our resident robin sits on the greenhouse deck, giving me a contemptuous look. I have long known that he thinks my only purpose in life is to dig so he can grab the worms from the turned soil, but in the last year he's become so confident of his rights that he will actually come and scold me if he thinks I'm being lazy. I'm starting to feel like wildlife is ganging up on me!

The slow-worms are already hibernating. We turned the compost in September so they could settle into their winter quarters undisturbed, but there are at least six stones in the stepping stone path that, if lifted, would reveal a torpid slow-worm family: grey males and tawny females with the brighter juveniles twisted into the parental knot like gold running through copper and silver. We try not to do anything that will trouble them, as they are our favourite slug-control systems, but sometimes we do have to move slabs and we ease them up gently on one corner, to check if there are sleeping slow-worms underneath. If there are, we'll usually lower the slab again and work around it until April when the family will disperse for the summer.

6 November

I get a call from Celia and head round to her house, wondering what ambitious scheme she has in mind this time. My fear is well-founded.

'I'm going to mobilise The Exotics,' she says, as soon as she opens the door. 'We need to become a pressure group.'

I nod, handing her a tin of biscuits – if I want to get fed in Celia's house, the only way to do it is to supply the food myself. I'm not sure what Stefan survives on but I suspect he has a good supply of takeaway menus hidden somewhere.

'Pressure to what?' I ask, confident that The Exotics are, by definition, a pressure group – one evening with them left Stefan ready to explode and I have only encountered them in dribs and drabs, but each occasion was like being crushed under a heavy social weight.

'Royal Mail. We need stamps.'

I have the wild urge to offer to buy a dozen first-class stamps and donate them to the cause if it will end her quest but I know that can't be what she's talking about (worse luck!) so I brace myself.

'We need a set of commemorative stamps detailing the work seed conservers do.'

I nod slowly – it's a fair point.

'So we need to settle on six famous deceased seed conservers and six living ones, each to be illustrated with a specimen plant from the species they dedicated themselves to.'

'We?' I ask feebly, knowing where this is going and not liking it.

'The Exotics. Obviously I wouldn't put myself forward...' her blue eyes fix me with a stare that makes it clear that I will put her forward, or die, and I find that I have nodded for the third time, without any conscious volition on my part.

I can't work out which frightens me more: the idea of proposing Celia's head on a stamp to the rest of The Exotics, or the prospect of watching the in-fighting for the other five stamp portraits. Given that she's thinking of six living and six dead, I'm imagining scenarios in which living seed conservers scheme to kill off their rivals in order to get one of the coveted slots, telling their guilty consciences (if they have any) that said rival is a shoo-in for one of the 'deceased' stamps and that's what they would have wanted...

'Can I ask a question?' I'm amazed to hear myself speak, and when Celia grunts assent, I realise I'm going to be as interested to hear what comes out of my mouth as she is.

'Do you like The Exotics?'

For a long moment she stares at me. 'Of course not. Who could like The Exotics?'

'So why are you their Chair?'

'It's a natural progression. Obviously it's a prestigious role, a career move...'

'There's nothing natural about The Exotics,' I mutter under my breath, then, louder, 'But it's *not* your career, Celia. This is your hobby. Hobbies are what we do for fun. Are you having fun?'

She gives me a long Arctic, or maybe it's an Antarctic, glare, but I am used to that and just shiver absent-mindedly.

'What do you mean?' Her voice is icy too, but I am on safer ground now. I may be a horticultural village idiot but in some areas I know my stuff, and this is one of them.

'You know what I mean, Celia. You just don't want to face it. You know about plants but I know about workaholism and you're definitely falling into it. Again.'

There is a long pause while Celia tries to stare me down then she sighs and slumps into a chair.

'You're right. It's just...'

'I know.' I pat her shoulder. 'There always seems to be another mountain to climb to get the best view.'

She grimaces. 'It's all right for you...'

This is code for 'you've had a meaningful career and the fact that you footle about with allotments and books is fine for somebody who's already *done* things'. Celia doesn't often

talk about her work life, but there's clearly a reason she works from home and that Stefan, every so often, becomes masterful and sends her off to Italy for several weeks to stay with an old school friend. I don't think it's just that he gets sick of her cooking, or lack of it.

'Careers aren't everything,' I say, remembering how much I loathed commuting to London every day, and how it always seemed to me that no work-related achievement could measure up to digging the first new potatoes or harvesting fresh peas. 'Anyway, a career can only be measured by outside parameters, not inside ones.'

'What do you mean?'

What do I mean? I struggle to articulate the thought I've just had, and then realise there's a simpler way to put it. 'How difficult is it to become Chair of The Exotics?'

'Virtually impossible,' Celia tries not to smirk, but fails.

'So... how much more impressive would it be for you to give up the role because you were, well... underwhelmed by it?'

'Underwhelmed? Did you not hear how that man spoke to me about my *Tillandsias*? Did you fail to grasp the import of their boycott of my alpine extravaganza?'

I take a deep breath. 'But *they* don't know how *you* feel about it, Celia. If you told them that you were fed up with the lack of challenge The Exotics present, and that you found their unimaginative approach to be a... a drag anchor on your own horticultural achievements, they would think you were really the bee's knees.'

'Bee's knees!' Celia snorts. 'Who are you channelling: Joyce Grenfell?'

A cat lifts her head, decides she must have misheard, and lowers it again.

There's a long pause. Then Celia slaps her thighs and stands up. 'For an idiot,' she says, 'you make a lot of sense sometimes. Where's my phone?'

I hand it to her and then pause. 'In English, Celia.'

She crosses her eyes as she hits the speed-dial button, waits and then speaks slowly and clearly, 'This is Celia Marsik. I'm resigning with immediate effect as Chair of The Exotics – it's not living up to my expectations and the hidebound nature of the organisation is holding me back.'

She ends the call and turns to me. I applaud. Joyce Grenfell and Dawn French lift their heads again and then return to sleep.

'Now,' Celia says, dragging me out of my chair. 'Let's talk about getting a museum of agriculture established in the city centre...'

30 November

Fred told me, and I told OH and Celia, and Brenda heard it over the fence and told Felix, and Felix told Rachel and Steve. The committee already knew, of course, and Compact and Bijou heard it from them, as they tried, unsuccessfully, to arbitrate the couple's continuing allotment war. Compact arrived in his MGB and Bijou puffed up on his pushbike, each of them ostentatiously ignoring the other.

How other people heard I don't know, but they did, so when Maisie opens the allotment gate for the last time and begins the walk to her plot, there is a small crowd waiting for her.

I'm cold and miserable, and don't really know why I'm standing on the bare earth that was once Maisie's well-stocked allotment, except that I am marking the passing of an institution. Three generations of Maisie's family have worked this plot and we'd all expected that one of the lanky nephews she'd corralled into helping her in the summer holidays would have caught the allotment virus and taken it over from her. Nothing has prepared us, as a community, for the idea that when she left us, her plot would become a stranger's.

Yes, that's it! An allotment is much more than a place to grow fruit and vegetables, it's a community and a community is built, more than anything, out of the commitment each individual makes to their chosen spot and chosen activity which then builds into a greater sense of each individual's part in something bigger. Losing Maisie is so much more than just losing a friend, a fellow cultivator, and a great source of inspiration and support – we are losing her personality, stamped on the soil, and rooted in the cultural traditions of her family which shaped not just her plot, but the whole site. Felix's golden raspberries were filched (he said they had suckered through the fence, but nobody believed it) from Maisie. My beloved rhubarb crowns were split from her patch seven years earlier and moved from plot to plot with me, before we got a plot of our own. Lola – Rachel and Steve's little girl – watered their allotment with the same baby-sized zinc watering can that Maisie inherited from her dad, who was given it by his dad the first time he came to the plot. We are losing our history along with Maisie.

On this cold, dark, winter's morning we work largely in silence, pulling out her bean frames, lifting her raised beds, taking out the trellis fence that had sheltered her raspberry canes from the vicious south-easterlies that scour the plot. We stack the cracked, old terracotta pots she used to support her squashes and pumpkins. We fold the netting from her fruit cages. After a couple of hours, there is little left to remind us of Maisie: just a strawberry bed and rhubarb patch and a path up the middle of the plot that leads to a shed from which the bluebird window blind, the singing kettle and the radio permanently tuned to Radio 2 have already been removed.

Maisie walks down the path in her wellies, dispensing a last bit of advice to each of us. When she gets to Felix she folds her arms and frowns. 'All my life I've known you, and you're nothing but a rascal. It's about time you faced the truth about yourself – ask and ye shall be driven, it says in the Bible. So ask her.'

By the time I've digested this Gnostic pronouncement, she's given me a brusque hug and a packet of blueberry seeds saying, 'Those books of yours are all right, but remember you can always fall back on your plot, as long as it's not into the raspberries.'

Before I can respond she's gone, down the path, handing her gate key to the committee chairman, off the plot and out of our lives without even a backward glance. She climbs into Mr Maisie's car and they drive away. As I wave goodbye I have the oddest feeling that some tin cans and old shoes, or at least some flowerpots and wellington boots, should have been tied to the back of the vehicle.

Sowing and growing

- **Garlic** can be planted any time from now until the traditional date of 21 December, the longest day. Garlic needs a prolonged period of cold weather to form cloves, so as soon as the temperature drops, you can get it started. If your soil is heavy and wet, there's a risk that garlic may rot, so add sand to the soil before planting out the cloves if you didn't do work through the summer to lighten the soil and make it friable.

- Early hardy **peas** can be sown outdoors now. Hardy peas are round and firm, and we like meteor and douce Provence for their flavour. If you have a rodent problem, sowing peas outdoors in winter is usually just a laborious and time-consuming way of feeding mice, but if you don't suffer from this kind of pest, early hardy peas will create solid root systems through the winter and belt off in spring, making an early crop for you.

Crop care and allotment tasks

Dig up a **rhubarb** crown and bring it into the house or shed for champagne rhubarb. This is a crop that is ready about the same time that people start to force outdoor rhubarb, so you can be eating lovely tender rhubarb when your neighbours are still thinking about getting theirs started. Pot your chosen crown into a really big pot or even an old dustbin and put another, bigger, light-excluding container over the top. It will need watering every fortnight and if placed in a south-facing location you will be able to harvest a good crop by the end of February, or by mid to late March in less ideal conditions. When you've taken your rhubarb (you'll only get one or two cuts of slender, pastel pink stems) replant the crown, ideally near your compost bin, and let it have a couple of years' rest and relaxation, as forcing takes a lot from the plant. Putting it near the compost bin means that the crown gets first shot at any run-off nutrients from the decomposing plant matter in the bin, which helps rebuild its strength. Don't cut stems from the plant for two years, or it may die. After that it will be back to full strength again.

Check your stored **chicory** (**endive**) and water if necessary before covering again.

Crops to harvest

- **Cabbages** and **cauliflowers**
- The last of the **celery** and **celeriac**
- **Chard**
- **Endive**
- **Jerusalem artichokes**
- **Kai-lan**
- **Leeks**
- **White Lisbon onions**

Recipe of the month:

Maple baked borlotti beans

500 g of dried borlotti beans, soaked overnight
2 tbsp olive oil
2 medium onions, roughly chopped
6 tbsp tomato ketchup (home-made if you have it)
1 tsp mushroom ketchup
2 tbsp maple syrup
1 tbsp caster sugar for light beans, 1 tbsp soft brown sugar for dark beans
1 tbsp wholegrain mustard
2 large bay leaves
1 tsp fresh thyme or ½ tsp dried
around 150 g bacon or end of gammon joint, chopped (optional)

Pre-heat slow cooker with just enough oil in the bottom to coat it thinly – beans can sometimes stick if the slow cooker isn't oiled.

Drain beans and boil for 30 minutes. Drain again.

Put 1 tbsp olive oil in a frying pan and add the onions. While frying them until translucent, mix ketchups, mustard, maple syrup and sugar with a cup or so of boiling water and pour into the slow cooker. Tip in the beans.

When the onion is starting to become translucent, add bay leaves and bacon, if you're using it, and cook for 3 minutes.

Tip into the slow cooker and stir to mix into the beans, adding the thyme at this point. If you have a dual setting cooker, it's 30 minutes on high and six to eight hours on low. For a single setting cooker it's usually five to seven hours.

Serve with crusty bread. Pleases four very hungry people.

Optional extras

Use chilli-infused oil instead of plain olive for warming beans!

For dinner parties, add a handful of green olives and half a handful of sun-dried tomatoes in the last hour of cooking. Put into bowls; sprinkle parmesan on top and grill briefly to create a delicious cheese crust.

Hints and tips

Check at the three-hour point, the first time you cook these beans, to see if there is enough liquid. It all depends on the quality of seal in your pot and the temperature it cooks at. If the beans look dry, add more boiling water, if they look a bit runny, lift the lid for the last hour by putting a wooden spoon in the pot and putting the lid back on so the steam can escape.

Borlotti baked beans are wonderful eaten cold with barbecued meats and leftovers can be liquidised with vegetable stock to make a hearty soup.

WINTER

December

1 December

Harvesting holly is one of my most and least favourite December tasks. Most favourite because it's a way to get a 'crop' from the allotment that saves me a small fortune: a holly wreath in our local Christmas market costs at least £20 while mine, made of an old sack wrapped around a wire coat hanger OH shaped into a circle for me, costs exactly nothing, is twice as fat and berried as the ones on sale, and is fun to make.

Least favourite because of what happened today and has happened every year since we moved to The Voodoo Plot. Some swine has poached most of my holly! I don't know who it is, and if I ever find out... well, let's say they won't be having a very merry Christmas.

The first year I made allowances – maybe they didn't realise that the new plot owners would want the holly; after all, the plot had been neglected for years so it was good that somebody, anybody, was making use of some of its harvest. The second year was annoying: it was clear the plot was in full cultivation and whoever cut the holly knew fine and well that they were nicking somebody else's stuff!

Today, as I walk up the main path towards The Voodoo Plot, I can feel a fury build in me – I don't feel peace and goodwill to anybody because the dark green, red-berry studded hedge that fronts one side of our plot is no longer red-berry studded. The thief has struck again! Sure enough, when I get up close, there are clean cuts through all the previously berry-laden branches. OH told me to cut the holly last week, but Maisie taught me to cut the materials for a wreath on 1 December and I don't like the idea of having to change my behaviour to forestall a thief, so in addition to anger at the theft I'm feeling stupid for ignoring his good advice.

I snap some pictures with my mobile phone and stomp off to find a committee member, but on my way I hear what sounds like wailing. I'm always aware that one of our stalwarts once broke his leg on the plot and lay for several hours until he was found so I head off in the direction of the sounds.

What I find is Compact, crouched against the fence that bisects their plot, crying like a little boy. As I run down the path to find out what's wrong, I register that there's something different about their plot, but I'm so concerned with his misery that I don't stop to take in what's happened. He clings to me, almost shaking me with the intensity of his grief. I pat his back, looking over his head at the plot, and slowly I grasp the situation. All their kitsch statues are missing: the concrete gnome tea party that has, from time to time, been classed as an obscene display, has disappeared; the wonderful 1950s tin advertisements that were nailed to their shed have been ripped away, leaving pale rectangles on the wooden walls; the astonishing ceramic fairy sculptures, imported from Germany, that they've given each other every anniversary for the past five years – vanished.

Compact wails aloud, 'I only came up to get some artichokes! What's Barry going to say?'

It takes a moment for me to click that Barry is Bijou, I'm so used to their nicknames. I continue to pat Compact's back, while easing my phone out of my back pocket and scrolling through to find Bijou's mobile number. It's difficult to text with one hand but I manage to send out an emergency message that I hope will cause him to come running, and then return to my job of comforting his partner.

Soon enough Bijou appears, cycle clips still in place, and begins to run down the path towards us. He slows, looks left and right, taking in the emptiness of the plot, and then speeds up again, almost bashing me out of the way.

'Are you OK?' He grabs Compact and begins to chafe his hands. 'Were you here? Did you try to stop them? Have they hurt you?'

I ease my way back down the path but for all the notice they take I could have marched off banging a big drum. As I turn the corner I can hear them both talking at once: and they are both apologising.

14 December

I find myself standing in the kitchen, glaring at the garlic. As usual at this time of year I have a choice: eat the garlic or plant the garlic. We never quite seem to plant enough, although each year we pretty well double the amount of garlic we put in the ground. Shop garlic never tastes as good as home-grown, but if I cook the garlic in my hand we may not have enough cloves to plant for next year, and that means buying in planting garlic, which is annoying. Cook or sow? Sow or cook? OH rescues me from my dilemma by walking past and grabbing the garlic from my hand to put in his pocket. Sow!

20 December

I'm at the plot in a drizzle, planting the garlic. I am cold, wet and miserable and every time I look up I see a wall of dense green – the holly bush without a single berry left on it. I try to console myself with thoughts of all the lovely garlic we will be able to eat next year but I feel like Scrooge McGarlic – I just want more of everything without the effort. Above all I don't want to be crouching in this cold not-quite-rain, trying to finish the planting before it gets dark.

As I straighten my back and sigh, Felix appears at the end of the main path, walking like a man taking part in an egg and spoon race. His eyes fixed on what is in front of him, he walks towards me and I drift down the path, unable to resist finding out what he's doing. To my amazement he opens the gate and walks up The Voodoo Plot path towards me. Felix has never visited our plot before! As he gets closer there's an amazing smell and I realise he's carrying a barbecue rack filled with roasted chestnuts which he sets down on top of our incinerator bin with a huge sigh.

'Eat up,' he gestures to the hot food.

I don't wait to be asked twice, I just rip off my muddy gloves and start peeling the red-hot nuts, juggling them from hand to hand because they are burning my fingertips.

''On't oo want 'ome?' My allotment manners are appalling. I'm speaking with my mouth full and fanning my hand in front of my face simultaneously because the food is burning its way down my oesophagus, but even as I speak I'm trying to peel another chestnut one-handed because they taste so good!

'I've had mine.' He smiles at me and I grin back. The hot food is working a miracle: I feel like I could stay here and plant garlic all day. Of course, as soon as I stop to think, bells start ringing in my head – this is Felix, giving me something for nothing, and that's never a straightforward proposal. There has to be a catch, a twist, a scam, a… something. I put down the chestnut I'm holding and give him a stern look, or as stern as I can manage with a volcanically molten mouthful.

'What's this about?' I ask, as soon as I can speak.

He shrugs. 'The Daughters were waiting for me when I got back from the plot last night. Apparently the Mother Superior suggested they needed to be forgiving and so they brought me a sack of nuts from the convent wood. I just thought…'

My mouth is hanging open. Felix appears to be having a Scrooge moment of his own. He shrugs again, looking embarrassed.

I grab the barbecue grill with my gloves and tip half the chestnuts into an empty flowerpot – I can't believe this generosity of spirit will last, so I'm going to take maximum advantage of it.

'Thanks,' I say, pointing him back down the path with his barbecue. 'I'm sure there are a few other hardy types around who would like a little treat.'

He nods. 'Compact and Bijou are up, decorating their plot. I'm taking some nuts up for them next.'

I return to planting garlic, shaking my head at the transformations that occur when I least expect them. I can't wait to see what Compact and Bijou have done: giant inflatable reindeer and a glow-in-the-dark Santa, probably. And even more than that, I can't wait to see the committee's reaction. If only I could find the holly poacher, I'd have a very happy Christmas indeed.

The mysteries of garlic

Garlic needs a long growing season. The old adage 'plant on the longest day and harvest on the shortest' is largely true. However, for several years, the general dampness and low average sunlight levels in the UK during the 'summer' (as we have to call it, because it's the bit between spring and autumn!) has meant that harvesting garlic has been problematic, because they haven't performed as usual.

Planting on 21 December is a good rule of thumb, though: it's a nice tradition to establish and it allows you to get up to the plot and harvest some new potatoes for Christmas Day lunch.

As well as at least 30 days of cold weather in the early weeks, garlic needs sun and fertility to perform well. We rake in a small amount of granular fertiliser before we plant out garlic, because it's a crop that almost never needs to be watered, hence you can't feed it with liquid fertilisers.

Prepare the soil well. Garlic easily gets swamped by weeds in the early months of growth, so ensure you've removed perennial weeds and can hoe or hand-weed around each garlic clove to remove annual weeds as they spring up.

Buy horticultural garlic. The stuff you buy to eat may have been treated to prevent it growing and is also often an imported variety that will not grow well in our mild damp winters. Solent Wight is a good white garlic, red Wight has the better flavour but doesn't store as well – both have been bred for UK growers. Once you have grown your own garlic, you can save bulbs to plant the following year.

Your purchased garlic arrives as a bulb, and you need to divide it with your fingers without piercing the cloves with your nails, which lets in mould and can cause rot. Plant each clove just below the surface (don't push it into the soil, make a shallow scrape and sit the clove with the end where it was attached to the bulb down, and the more pointy end up and then pull the soil back around it with your fingers) and about 15–18 centimetres apart to allow hoeing room. Rows should be at least 30 centimetres apart. We now allow 40 centimetres between rows, as rust has become such a problem on garlic and close planting encourages its spread.

You may need to stop birds pulling up the cloves. Many people advocate horticultural fleece. I believe (with no evidence to back me up) that this may encourage rust to remain in the soil around the cloves and I'm sure it reduces the risk of frost, which actually helps garlic grow, so we stick twigs in the soil and link them with brightly coloured string. This stops birds landing but allows 'soil hygiene' to take place as winter frosts and snow break up the soil surface and kill any lurking bacteria, mould, fungal spores and other nasties. As I've said, garlic needs prolonged cold to make fat bulbs, so hope for a winter than contains a month of frost!

Don't water until spring, and only then if it's really dry weather. Don't water once the bulbs begin to look large and round as they will rot quickly if they have too high a water content.

If flowers form – and it's rare that they do – cut them off with a pair of scissors.

Harvest around late June (if you're lucky) or July if the weather's been cold and damp. The idea is to lift when the leaves begin to turn yellow and die back. My experience is that rust gets hold of the garlic before this happens, and it will damage the plant once it really gets a hold so usually we end up lifting because of the rust, not because the plant looks ready. Dispose of leaves and roots by burning or in the rubbish bin if you have rust – composting will just spread the rust throughout your soil. Don't grow any alliums (garlic, onions, leeks, shallots) in the same place two years running and leave it three years between allium crops if you have experienced rust.

Watch out for onion white rot. It manifests as something very like the plants being ready to lift, in that the leaves turn yellow, but in healthy plants the leaves become dry and papery, whereas onion white rot turns them damp and slimy. Often when you lift them up you will see fluffy white material around the roots. The only solution to this problem is not to grow any alliums in that area for eight to ten years. We tend to sow a green manure (usually phacelia) as soon as we lift the garlic, dig it into the soil in autumn, and in January or February go over the area with a weed burner before turning it over with a fork again. This ensures the soil has been enriched with some bulky matter to improve drainage and fertility and that persistent fungal spores have been disturbed (and hopefully, cremated!).

Elephant garlic is actually more like a leek and seems to have a higher natural resistance to onion white rot. Grow it like ordinary garlic, but plant cloves around 25 centimetres apart and in rows 45 centimetres apart. It may produce a tall flower spike, but as soon as you spot this, snip the flower head off. It doesn't affect the keeping qualities of the garlic but if you let it flower the plant will focus on flower production, rather than producing cloves. A successful elephant garlic will produce five or six cloves, four to six times the size of standard garlic cloves. These are delicious when roasted or smoked but much milder than traditional garlic.

All garlic varieties should be lifted, set on wire trays or other air-circulating devices, and have their roots trimmed off. Give the bulbs several weeks in a cool, airy place to dry completely, trim back the leaves and then plait them or otherwise store them to use through the year. Remember that damp will make them rot very quickly.

Sowing and growing

Start some **pak choi** and **mizuna** in troughs in a cold greenhouse. You can cover the troughs with glass or plastic to give them extra protection. Growing slowly through the next three months, they will provide a few baby veg in the hungry gap in March and April.

Crop care and allotment tasks

Give all the plants that need it some winter protection. Cover **strawberry** beds with fleece to keep the sharp frosts away, and if your **asparagus** is at all exposed, consider giving it the same treatment – frost can cause damage to the growing tips of the spears while they are underground, so that next year's crop has a distorted shape and a woody texture.

Crops to harvest

- **Cabbages, kale, Brussels sprouts** and **winter cauliflowers**
- **Carrots**
- **Celery** and **celeriac**
- This is the time to start bringing your containers of **chicory** (**endive**) into a warmer environment (ours go into the glass porch in front of the house, or the unheated greenhouse on the plot) and water them before covering them again. You'll have dense heads of chicory to eat in 21–28 days.
- **Jerusalem artichoke**
- **Kohlrabi**
- **Leeks**
- **Parsnip** and **swede**
- **Red cabbage**
- **Salsify** and **scorzonera**
- **Spinach (perpetual), leaf beet** and **chard**
- **Turnip**
- **Winter density lettuce**

Recipe of the month:

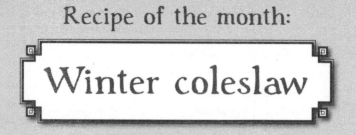

Winter coleslaw

This recipe is ideal for using up the red cabbages that are often lurking on the winter allotment, and offers a range of substitutions so that most allotment-holders can cobble together a great-tasting and healthy dish from what they have on hand. The basic recipe is made 24 hours in advance with the final additions being made just before it reaches the table.

Either half a red onion, very finely chopped or two shallots ditto, or a half a leek halved lengthways and finely sliced
A red cabbage, outer leaves removed, white heart cut away, the remainder either finely sliced or shredded
75 g chopped walnuts, lightly toasted, or cobnuts, chopped and toasted
Around 1 tbsp parsley (move it into your greenhouse in the winter, it will continue to grow slowly) or twice the amount of chopped mizuna
4 tbsp walnut oil or tarragon-infused olive oil (use wide-necked jars in which you soak sprigs of French tarragon for six weeks, shaking gently every day to encourage the tarragon to flavour the olive oil)
3 tbsp balsamic vinegar
1 tbsp maple syrup
1 tsp wholegrain mustard

1 stored apple (skin left on), cored and finely chopped
½ tsp lemon juice

Stir together the allium of your choice and the cabbage and nuts with half the parsley/mizuna.

In a jar, shake together oil, vinegar, syrup and mustard and pour over the vegetables and nuts. Mix well.

Cover and refrigerate overnight. Next day, toss the coleslaw again and mix together the rest of the parsley/mizuna with the apple and lemon juice. Garnish the top of the coleslaw with this mixture and serve.

This coleslaw is really good served in pitta breads as part of a winter lunch box. In that case, put the apple mixture in a small container to be shaken into the pitta bread just before eating.

January

5 January

For Christmas I get a beautiful stainless steel trowel with a maple handle. There were many years when my gifts were aspirational: books about growing fruit and veg and tubs and planters that allowed me to pretend I was growing my own food on a real, rather than pretend, scale. Now, most of my presents relate to digging, planting or storing crops and I'm thrilled to bits by the sheer practical elegance of forks and dibbers, trugs and rakes. I'm 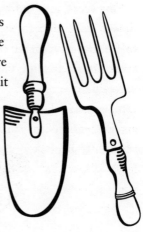 also desperate to try out my new implement, but it isn't going to be of any use until spring, so I'm reduced to standing it against the wall and gazing at it, but OH has fallen over it three times since Christmas day so my trowel and I have been banished to the plot, along with a hammer and a nail so that I can locate a suitable place on the shed wall to hang my new treasure.

New Year's resolutions are not my thing, but I usually make an August resolution to plant potatoes in an outdoor container that gets relocated in October to the unheated greenhouse. It means we have new potatoes for Christmas Day lunch. This year we grew potatoes in two big canvas planters in the greenhouse allotment and my trip to the plot has allowed me to find time to tip the compost out of the second one and pull fist-sized creamy-coloured spuds from the soil. We've gone for Yukon gold this year, and the egg-shaped tubers look like Christmas decorations as I brush away the dry earth and pop them into a trug to take home and boil for dinner.

Next week we'll start planting seeds in this greenhouse, so it's time to make space for seed trays and potting compost. I'm starting to feel the excitement of the growing year ahead, and also the smug satisfaction of the organised vegetable grower who harvests, for pennies, what other people are spending vast sums to obtain. What I love most about the winter potatoes is that they have the same taste and texture as spring-grown new potatoes, so that the darkest winter days are enlivened by the pure taste of spring.

I really want to brag about our perfectly formed spuds, and my feet naturally turn towards Maisie's plot. I am halfway to her shed before I realise, yet again, that Maisie won't be there. It's taking me a long time to accept that she's really gone. Actually, I'm not accepting it at all – unless I'm really thinking clearly, I have a homing instinct for Maisie's practical good sense and down-to-earth view of the world, not to mention the occasional convoluted misuse of language that could keep me both amused and entertained during a long afternoon's planting, hoeing or harvesting.

Lola received a Christmas postcard from Maisie and Mr Maisie, posted from the cruise ship on which they were visiting the Caribbean and learning, as Maisie put it, to dance the Pasa Noblé, but nobody else has heard a word from her.

Of course, halfway to Maisie's old plot is also halfway to Felix's, so I carry on, heavy-hearted, and push my way through the various bits of paraphernalia that make his allotment look more like a junk yard and less like a growing space every week. Released from Maisie's surveillance, Felix has become completely undisciplined and while we're all delighted that Brenda is still around, having spent the summer surreptitiously peddling her hydroponic tomatoes into fruit, it's worrying to see how much weird equipment he's amassing. Soon he'll be competing for Compact and Bijou's unofficial title of 'allotment that looks least like an allotment'.

His shed also seems to be empty so I turn to leave, and then hear a peculiar sound from behind the shed, where Celia and I once braved the nettles: well, Celia braved them, I wimped about in them! I put down my trug of spuds and wander round the corner.

Balaclava-clad Felix, who has never been seen to do anything remotely athletic, is sitting on Brenda's bicycle, mounted in its electricity-generating rig, peddling like a maniac. This alone is staggering, but there is then some kind of contraption that attaches to a small galvanised bin with holes punched in it, the contents of which are glowing cherry-red. There's actually heat haze rising from both the bin and Felix.

After a moment of sheer confusion, I turn and head back to my trug, selecting two perfect potatoes and holding them up, one in each hand, as I step into Felix's line of vision. Puffing and panting, he nods, and I gingerly lean over the bin and lay the spuds on the grill above the grey and red charcoal, feeling my face tighten immediately as the heat reaches me.

After about ten minutes his peddling slows and he takes off the balaclava.

'I reckon that will cook five kilos of chestnuts over the next two hours, now it's reached temperature,' he says proudly.

'So?' I say. 'Not that it's not an impressive achievement but… so?'

Felix frowns. 'It's entrepreneurship,' he says. 'I'm going to take it around all the industrial estates, and down to the seafront, and maybe into the Lanes, and sell bags of hot chestnuts. Maybe spuds too, if yours cook OK. And in summer I can rig it to a belt and make pedal-power smoothies instead of using the bellows mechanism to heat the coals.'

I nod, unenthusiastically. I'm as keen on roasted chestnuts as the next person but the idea of Felix pedalling around the city with a dustbin full of red-hot coals strikes me as unlikely to gain civic approval. There's another problem too.

'Don't you need a licence and food hygiene training and insurance and – '

He makes a rude noise. 'Not if they don't catch me.'

I turn the potatoes over with my gloved hand, to avoid continuing the conversation. Once again, Felix has had a great idea and is about to turn it into a scam. He's learnt nothing from his experience with the Daughters of Retribution. Then I find I'm grinning. It's true: nothing's changed – Maisie's not here to offer one of her malapropisms, but the world is continuing and Felix is doing what he's always done. Like the cycles of growth and harvest, he's bounced back from failure into full-blown villainy and that's oddly comforting. He's as reliably unreliable as a packet of favourite but temperamental seeds!

17 January

I'm out shopping and I see somebody I vaguely recognise. This happens a lot: on an allotment site with several hundred tenants it's common to 'sort of' know lots of people, at least to nod to as I pass, but not really know anything more about them than that they have a good way with cauliflowers, or I wouldn't swap my redcurrants for theirs, or whatever... basically, I know people by their plots, not their faces or where they work. I have a routine for this situation, which is to nod and say 'nice weather for it' which can be taken satirically or at face value, whatever the weather, and the allotment-holder in question can then tell me which crop it is or isn't nice weather for in their view, and we'll have had a 'nice' conversation without me ever having to admit I don't know their name.

But this time, as I start to say my platitude, I realise that the person in front of me is not an allotment-holder, it's an ex-allotment-holder. It's Jeremy; Jeremy of the formerly excellent greenhouse; Jeremy the lemongrass lover. My words trail off. Is it good form to mention his plot? Should I ask if he's had a letter of termination? Perhaps he just needs a little encouragement to get back into the swing of growing things – and it is January, after all, the season of good resolutions. Before I can work out a suitably inspiring way to get him back to the plot, he takes the initiative, smiling uneasily at me and then looking straight past me, waving at somebody behind me.

'Nice to see you!' his false bonhomie is so thickly laid on that he could have got a job as Father Christmas a couple of weeks ago. 'Would *love* to stop and chat, but that's a friend of mine over there, must dash!'

He zooms past me, still waving wildly. After a moment I turn round. Jeremy is fast-walking into the distance, all alone. Clearly he's no longer an enthusiastic plot-holder and nor is he willing to talk about why.

I shake my head as I continue on my way – people give up growing their own for all kinds of reasons, and it's entirely up to them whether they want to have an allotment or not. I do have strong feelings about people who just drift away, though... it's really difficult for the many thousands of folk, up and down the country, who are desperate to try growing their own food, and who see neglected plots sitting idle. It can take up to six months for many councils to send a letter to absent allotment tenants, and if the tenant appeals, a further six months for the situation to be resolved. That's a year of growing and eating that some other family has been denied – and while I fully appreciate that life can, and does, get in the way of allotments, and that most people are not as dedicated (fanatical, perhaps?) as I am, it still bugs me that they don't have the courtesy to write to the council and hand back their plot, when it becomes clear they can't or won't be tending it, so that somebody else can have the fun of cultivating it.

22 January

I have a date with Celia. We sit at my dining table – the kitchen one isn't big enough – and lay out all our seeds for the year ahead.

Every year we do this; it's like a gigantic game of Happy Families, except that we both end up happy.

Celia announces a family name, '*Cucurbitaceae*', and I scramble through the fanned-out packets, picking out each pumpkin, squash, gourd, cucumber, melon and marrow in my collection. Celia is doing the same with hers. We end up with a handful of packets each and then get to decide if we want to exchange any of the seeds we've got. I score an excellent small 'dish' squash – the kind that you can cut the top off, scoop the seeds out, bake whole in the oven and then fill with cheese and rice or a thick spicy soup to make a meal and a bowl in one. Celia begs for some of my outdoor cucumber seeds as she wants to make pickled gherkins. I give her the seed with a mental note that I will probably end up pickling the cucumbers for her – last time she tried making preserves Stefan lived on antacid tablets for six months.

She gives me a smug smile. 'What else is in the *Cucurbitaceae* family?'

I shrug, scouring my collection, and hers, to try to spot what I've missed.

'Loofahs,' she says grandly, spinning a pack of seed into the middle of the table like the Ace of Spades.

I am suitably amazed.

'Are you going to try to grow them?' The back of the packet says the seed needs 110 days of sun. It doesn't seem likely in the UK, but Celia is undaunted.

'Of course I'll grow them,' she says, and it's not a boast. She will. Because they are not an edible, I have only a passing interest in this project, but I'm pretty sure I know what Celia's friends and family will be getting for Christmas next year – loofahs!

I pass on the loofah seeds and it's my turn to choose.

'*Solanaceae*,' I say.

Celia nods slowly. It's a good family, containing, as it does, the *Brugmansia* or angel's trumpet, which has the most wonderfully scented flower in the world, its cousin the *Datura* from which Amazonian tribes make poison darts, the tomato, the potato and deadly nightshade.

'This could take a while,' she announces as she starts to gather up seed packets.

I go and put the kettle on. As I wait for it to boil, I start to think of how I'm going to explain all the new additions to our planting scheme to OH, who will be quietly infuriated to find he already has to make room for another kind of squash, given that we have planned to plant three different varieties of this astonishingly rambling and intrusive plant. Still... his annoyance is only ever momentary and I'm sure he'll love the new plants when he hears how tasty they all are.

'Are you staying for dinner?' I yell to Celia. Silly question. Of course she is.

'Stupid question,' she yells back. 'Of course I am.'

I pull open the root box and see what we've got to eat. Celeriac, swede, and some of the lovely Christmas new potatoes that we tipped out of their containers last month.

'Subversive gratin?' I yell.

'Sounds good,' she yells back, and while the tea brews I lay out the ingredients for dinner.

25 January

I have a plethora of new seeds, and I seem to remember having promised OH that I wouldn't buy any more seeds until we'd either planted, or disposed of, all the seeds we currently have. But somebody told me about an amazing tomato they grew this summer and I want to try it for myself, and we definitely need more broad beans so there's no harm looking through just one catalogue…

Two and a half hours later I seem to have ordered 16 packets of seed. There are definite downsides to the Internet and one is that in the old days it was necessary to walk to the postbox with an order form from a paper catalogue, or to ring somebody up and to read a seed order out to them, both of which tended to act as a common-sense filter. But on the Internet you can send your order in seconds, without any need to stop and reflect on where you're going to put the plants if they grow.

I decide it's time to go to the plot and do some digging. I'm going to have to adjust our planting scheme for next year and the best way to do that is to go and have a look at what's possible.

Sowing and growing

- **Cauliflowers** sown in the greenhouse now are called summer cauliflowers – plant them out in April and be eating them in July.
- **Chillies** need the longest possible growing season and also need lots of heat, so this is a seed to start in a heated propagator or on the kitchen windowsill.

- **Onions** can be started from seed in January – onions from seed can be pernickety and one way to get them going is with bottom heat in an electric propagator in January, planting out around March or April. Once they sprout, lower the heat but keep the sunlight levels up and don't overwater. The advantage of growing onions from seed is that it's a much cheaper way than buying sets. The disadvantage is that they are more inclined to bolt.

- **Oriental leaves** – the mustards in particular are good started now and eaten really early, before they become too hot and too leathery to be used as salad greens. We grow ours in troughs in the greenhouse and cut as much as we want with scissors. Germination isn't brilliant and growth is slow, but home-grown baby leaves are exciting to the palate, cost-effective and environmentally friendly compared to buying forced salad leaves from a supermarket.

- **Sweet peas** – we grow them because they encourage so many beneficial insects and because the smell is heavenly. I always plan to overwinter them, but never remember to, so we start ours in an unheated greenhouse in January with a sheet of glass over the tray of compost they are sown in. Remember to remove the glass before the seedlings touch it. Our seed is saved from many years of allotment growing, so it's well used to our local conditions. If you have seed you've purchased, it may need a heated greenhouse or propagator.

Crop care and allotment tasks

Get the greenhouse ready for the sowing season ahead: make sure you've dealt with any draughts and that everything is both clean and sterile. We now use vinegar to kill weeds rather than anything else – it seems to work as well as shop-bought formulations and at least we know what's in it. Spray weeds with 50/50 water and white vinegar – best done on dry days, which seems to aid in the effectiveness of the vinegar.

If you have overwintering **onion** sets in the ground, this is a good time to give them a nitrogen-rich feed in granular form. Some people like to use poultry pellets but we generally go for granulated sulphate of ammonia, because we can be sure it has the right level of nitrogen. Sprinkled on, according to packet instructions, and then lightly raked into the soil around the onions with a gloved hand, it really promotes top growth when spring arrives and also, apparently can stop the onions bolting. Some people rake or hoe their winter onion feed into the ground, but over the years I've found that cold weather and hand-to-eye coordination do not mix, and I've chopped too many onions with a hoe, or raked them out of the soil, to take that risk. Onions are just a manual crop, in my experience!

Check stored **potatoes** and **onions** to be sure there is no rot, and dispose of any split or damaged tubers or bulbs before infection spreads to the rest of your stock.

Order seeds – but only after sorting through your current stock and arranging swaps with allotment neighbours or friends. You may find you can source a lot of seeds through swaps or just splitting a packet of seeds with a neighbour, thus reducing costs and wastage.

Crops to harvest

- **Cabbages, kale, beet** and **chard** will be going strong.
- **Jerusalem artichokes**
- **Leeks**
- **Mooli**
- **Parsnips** and **swedes**. Parsnips are better after the first frost, and you might want to cover both roots with a fleece canopy to stop them freezing solid. There are few things more frustrating than spending eight to ten months growing a crop only to find that on the one day you want to dig it up and take it home, it's locked into a bed of ice!
- **Winter density salad leaves**, especially those grown under cover.

Recipe of the month:

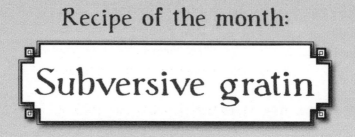

Subversive gratin

There was a time when OH and I knew some people who were definitely on the fringes of society. They were nice people and we enjoyed their company but sometimes their ideas were decidedly strange and counter-culture. Their food was sometimes odd too: not just vegan odd (which is definitely mainstream now) or macrobiotic odd, but really, really odd. We once knew a guy who would only eat certain foods when the moon was waxing or waning; his diet was a little like moon planting cycles but with what was on his plate rather than in the ground. There were some fantastic meals, though – the first time we ever ate celeriac was with a bunch of animal rights activists who went on to have a very murky history indeed. I'm glad we didn't spend much time with them, as several went to prison, but I've always been grateful for the introduction the subversives gave me to their gratin.

Around a kilo of well-washed potatoes, unpeeled – try to pick ones that are similar in size
Squeeze of lemon juice
1 small celeriac
1 small swede
4 medium-sized carrots
1 tbsp olive oil
60 g butter

3 garlic cloves, or one elephant garlic clove, crushed or minced
Fresh thyme
Fresh tarragon
100 ml boiling water or hot vegetable stock

Thinly slice the potatoes, dropping them into a bowl of cold water with a squirt of lemon juice in it to stop them browning. Repeat the process with the celeriac and swede, peeling them first and then slicing them as thinly as you can manage, dropping each root vegetable into its own bowl of cold lemon water.

Thinly slice the carrot, peeling if necessary.

Preheat the oven to 190°C/ gas mark 5.

Heat the olive oil in a small pan, keeping the heat to medium so that when you add the garlic it doesn't brown. As the garlic becomes translucent, add the butter and shake to ensure it foams and blends with the garlic.

Keeping one eye on the pan, and shaking or stirring when necessary, strip the thyme leaves and the tarragon leaves from the stems and lightly chop the tarragon so it's a similar size to the thyme.

Throw the herbs in with the garlic, stir to coat with the butter/ oil mix and remove from the heat almost immediately – you just want to release the fragrance from the herbs, not brown them.

Brush a layer of the herb butter around the base and sides of a deep ovenproof dish.

Drain the spuds, celeriac and swede, patting them dry with clean tea towels or paper towels. Put a layer of the potatoes on the base of the dish, using about a quarter of the slices, and overlapping them slightly. Brush this layer with herb butter and sprinkle with pepper, then add all the celeriac, another layer of potato brushed with herb butter and lightly peppered, the carrot, then potato, butter and pepper, the swede and a final layer of potatoes and butter.

Firm the layers down well, gently pour the stock or water into the dish and brush the remaining butter over the top.

Cover with foil and cook for around 50 minutes to an hour or until the slices are tender to the point of a sharp knife or a skewer. Remove the foil and put the dish under a medium grill for a few minutes so that the top layers become crisp and golden.

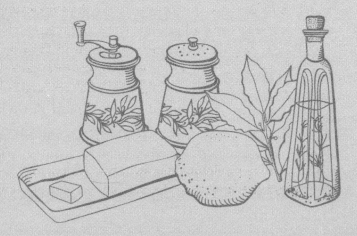

February

1 February

When does spring begin for an allotment-holder? It might seem like a moot point, but it's a source of some friction between me and Celia and between Celia and the world. You see, she's the kind of person who likes things to be definite. She definitely knows when the first day of spring is: 21 March, the vernal equinox – but equinoxes drift, like Easter, and that makes her unhappy. Add to her unhappiness the idea that the Met Office, in all other ways an utterly reliable source (according to Celia), pins the spring start date to 1 March, a decision with which OH concurs, and she becomes positively rattled. I am not a contributor to her unease because I have never told her what I believe. For me, spring starts on 1 February – the day, every year, when I plant my sweet pea seeds. I don't care what the heavens or the climate scientists say, sweet pea sowing day marks the beginning of spring, for me.

It's the day that the excitement really starts to build. I check I have enough seed trays for the year ahead, and enough of the various forms of compost necessary to get all my seeds started (I never do, I always run out of something!) and all the labels and plenty of pots to move my seedlings into... I become, in fact, obsessed.

The nature of my obsession is such that OH has, from time to time, suggested that we heat the greenhouse a bit more and turn the central heating off altogether, as I spend more time in the greenhouse in February than indoors. I ignore these comments. I am well aware that by April my greenhouse duties will be over and his will be beginning.

We have a clear division of labour – I sow things and get them to a reasonable size, and he takes over on the cultivation side. When a greenhouse crop goes from seedling to plant, it ceases to be my baby and becomes his project. So by the end of April, I only go into the greenhouses (yes, we have two!) if he can't get there, and I have clear instructions on what to turn, water, pick and prune, which I follow carefully. This means that, unlike a lot of allotment couples, we don't argue (much) about cultivation. OH is the authority on some things – lawns, structures, tools, greenhouse plants – while I am the expert on others – sowing, soft fruit, crop rotation, cooking – and where there is an area of mutual interest (tree fruit) we still divide the tasks rather than sharing them. I know there are couples who can labour alongside each other like Tom and Barbara in *The Good Life*, but that's not us: our harmony depends on clear demarcation between what OH does and what I do. As I stand in the greenhouse, smelling the glorious aroma of fresh seed compost and looking at the filled but un-germinated seed trays bursting with as yet unknown potential, I wonder if I should recommend a similar system to Compact and Bijou?

Maybe not. The last I heard, they were planning a tour of the Highlands after a spectacularly successful Burns Night celebration in which they cooked (or rather, burnt) haggis burgers on their allotment barbecue, drank copious amounts of whisky and began to recite the kind of poetry that would have got them an antisocial behaviour notice from any passing allotment officer – fortunately, the only passing person was Felix who helped them drink the whisky and was therefore in a position to confirm that neeps and tatties were eaten, toasts were made and general bonhomie ensued. Jerusalem artichokes were not on the menu.

12 February

The potatoes have arrived! I belt down to the shop to get first pick and end up coming home with more first earlies than I'd planned and more second earlies than we have room for. OH will despair, I know, and I still haven't told him about the 16 packets of seed that I've hidden in my underwear drawer for the right occasion to reveal that we're even richer in potential food crops than he thought. Once again I sit down with the crop rotation plan and spend an hour juggling and squeezing and altering and squashing things up until, in theory, there is just enough room on the plot to plant all the potatoes.

We've been saving egg cartons since the autumn, as these are the best things in which to place potatoes that need chitting and we've made space on the spare bedroom bookshelf for the cartons to sit. We start our potatoes later than we used to. February is early enough, given that the idea is to get good shoots on the seed potatoes, which takes about six weeks. We never plant out before mid March, so the January chitting we used to do was largely a waste of effort – old wives' tales and the folklore of the old guard should be measured against your own allotment successes and failures to see what really works. For years we started our potatoes off as soon as the Christmas holidays were over, and for years I ended up rubbing away shoots that had got too long because the weather wasn't good for planting, but I just didn't have the nerve to start the spuds later! Climate change and new varieties can really alter the way plants grow, so it's vital to be curious and open-minded about the growing routines we get into.

I stand each potato on end, with the more rounded end uppermost, in an egg carton. I'll turn the cartons every day and the cool light of the north-facing room will be just enough to get the shoots started without too much warmth, which makes them grow too vigorously.

At this point they look like a battalion of Humpty Dumpties and one year I drew little faces on them all, like the Tenniel illustration in *Alice Through the Looking Glass*, which had two negative effects: 1) every time I went into the room I thought their eyes were following me and 2) Celia said I might have poisoned the tubers so they would grow peculiarly because I used an indelible marker pen.

I'm happy to say that we've felt no ill effects from eating the many children the Humpty Dumpty parents produced but I still have nightmares about roomfuls of talking potato heads!

14 February

Valentine's Day. It's never been a big allotment day – Christmas Day is hardcore: that's when all the dedicated growers pitch up to their plots to harvest Brussels sprouts for the Christmas lunch table, and, if they're like us, new potatoes to serve with the roast meat. Harvest Festival is usually a biggie too: lots of sites have some kind of produce show or open day that takes place around harvest time. Easter's a pretty big deal on many sites, as that's potato-planting weekend for a lot of the old guard... but Valentine's Day? Not so much.

Until this year.

This year I am part of a project – a surprise for Bijou, organised by Compact. Actually, 'organised' is an inadequate word for what's going on. Compact has orchestrated, or maybe even impresarioed (if there is such a word) an event for his partner and it starts with me ringing Bijou and urging him to get to the allotment in a hurry.

This is why I'm standing in the middle of The Voodoo Plot on a drizzly February morning. My instructions have been very clear, even down to the fact that I mustn't bolt the gate onto the plot. 'Let it swing to and fro,' Compact has told me. 'It will add verisimilitude to the conversation.' Rain falling, gate swinging, female blackbird giving me the evil eye from the top of our neighbour's elderberry tree (the female blackbird often gives me the evil eye, it's noticeable that she will fly to the opposite side of the allotment to avoid me, but she stays put when OH approaches her. I think she's a floozy) – it couldn't be much more authentic as a horrible day in February unless I developed pneumonia as a result of this charade.

I'm worried that Bijou won't come out. After all, the weather is vile and like most allotment-holders at this time of year, he has few crops to worry about. The remaining Brussels sprouts, cabbages and kale are unlikely to be suffering any problems, and the purple sprouting hasn't really started yet. So will he really respond to my somewhat feeble attempt to get him to leave his cosy, centrally heated flat, with its two little Pomeranian dogs, Italian coffee maker, surround-sound TV, etc., to traipse down here and check out the state of his allotment?

If it was Felix or Celia, Rachel or Steve, I'd know the answer instantly. Maisie too, when she was with us, would have been up like a shot if there was any suggestion of a horticultural panic. But Bijou...? I'm not convinced he's going to play along.

When he answers my call I clear my throat, 'Um... I just came past your plot (why did I say that, there's no reason for me to be walking past his plot!) and it looks like there's a problem with your shed. I think you should come up and check it out...'

'Yes, right. Of course! Right! Well... does it look sort of... dangerous?'

I'd forgotten the thieves and their haul of ceramic kitsch: Compact and Bijou spent several weeks scouring eBay for traces of their purloined porcelain but never found any.

'No,' I reassure him. 'It just looks a bit odd.'

Actually the shed *is* occupied, by Compact, a jeroboam of champagne and 70 purple gladioli. 'Why purple?' I'd asked, as I helped him unload the flowers from the back of the MGB pulled up at the allotment gate.

'His favourite colour,' Compact replied, stuffing yet another bucketful of purple spires into a corner of the shed.

It was impressive, visually at least, and once the gas heater warmed the shed up a bit, I was sure it would be comfortable too, although the choice of music, *The Magic Flute*, seemed odd to me.

'It's his favourite,' said Compact, when I asked again, and his smirk suggested I might not want to enquire any further.

Now, 'I'm on my way,' Bijou squeaks into the phone and I trot down to Maisie's old plot and hide behind her shed, so that he can't find me if he decides he'd like reinforcements on his way to sort out whatever's happened to the allotment this time. Maisie's plot will be let to new tenants in March, and as I loiter, like an allotment pervert, I find myself idly kicking up a few weeds so that the new tenants don't have too much to do. Finally I'm beginning to accept that she's no longer around, and that new growers will make this space their own.

I watch the main path and soon enough I see him cycle by, muffled up in a Paddington Bear coat and a hat like a giant marshmallow which Compact's mother knitted him for Christmas.

I slope along in his wake, cutting through the plots, far enough behind not to be spotted but close enough to see and hear what happens.

Their shed door is flapping in the wind, rather like the gate on The Voodoo Plot. Bijou bustles up the path, from which both fences have been removed, and as he puts his hand on the latch, Mozart wells out and I guess Compact must have been watching from the window.

Even above the overture I hear Compact yell 'Surprise!' and see Bijou jump, literally, several inches in the air. For a moment I fear he'll have a heart attack, but a moment later he's clasping his hands and making those 'oh, oh, oh' sounds that people make when they are surprised, but also delighted, and I drift away, happy that our lovebirds are billing and cooing again.

Back on The Voodoo Plot I double check the gate is properly latched and give the old shed a stern look. 'You're next,' I tell it and it seems to lean even more drunkenly under the weight of the warning.

By the end of the summer I want to have a real shed, an asparagus bed, and new fruit trees that actually bear fruit. But for now, all I need to do is walk home in the rain. Another year of growing is just beginning and, whatever happens, it'll be exciting to see what we harvest.

Sowing and growing

- **Aubergines** – I find these to be a really tricky plant to grow well. February is the earliest I start them off, as I've had experience of sturdy seedlings outgrowing their strength. They just get spindly if they grow upwards before there's enough light to support sturdy stem development. They do need a heated propagator (around 21°C) but they don't like too much moisture with their heat and nor do they like their compost to dry out completely. Lower the heat once they germinate. We never plant out aubergines: they stay in the greenhouse all year and we do better with the miniature or small varieties than the full-sized versions which rarely produce truly substantial fruits for us.

- **Broad beans** can go in now if you don't plant yours in autumn; make sure you choose a spring-sowing variety.
- **Brussels sprouts**
- **Cabbages,** especially **red cabbage,** which thrives on an early start and likes to get into its final growing position before the heat of summer, so sowing now for an April planting usually works well.
- **Carrots** under a cloche – in our case, carrots in a container under a cloche, as we have clay soil, carrot fly and late frosts to contend with.
- This is the month to start fresh **lemongrass** on a kitchen windowsill. Buy stems of lemongrass, preferably organically grown, but in any case steep them in lukewarm water for an hour to wash away any chemicals that might be lurking on the surface, or any retardants used to inhibit sprouting, then sink them about 5 centimetres into a blend of 50 per cent standard potting compost, 50 per cent sand – we use plant-and-go-away propagators to get lemongrass established. Because it's a tropical grass, it needs good daylight, so give it lots of light in the early weeks, if necessary standing it on a white tile with a mirror behind it to reflect maximum light into the plant.
- Early varieties of **lettuce** and **radish** can be sown in large pots or trays in the greenhouse – we do particularly well with **Little Gem** sown in February. A pot of **rocket** will be wonderfully peppery if sown in the greenhouse now, covered with glass or even cling film until the plants are around an inch tall.
- **Onions** from seed should be started now. They need about 15°C to get them going so you may be best off using the windowsill in a cool room to start them off.

- Sow **pak choi** in a tray in the cold greenhouse, and cover the container with a glass or plastic propagator lid. In a couple of months you should have baby pak choi with an extremely tender consistency.
- **Peas** of the first early variety planted now will hit the ground running and sprint away – they are really hardy for vegetables with such a tender flavour.
- **Summer cabbages**
- **Tomatoes, peppers** and **chillies** can be started in a heated greenhouse or heated propagator or on a warm south-facing windowsill – be sure that you're going to be able to pot them on and keep them warm enough, though. More plants get checked through being started too early than fail to produce through being started too late, in my experience.
- **Turnips,** especially if you want to harvest baby turnips.

Crop care and allotment tasks

February is a good month to finish **digging** as the weather (rain, wind and frost) is for once the grower's friend – it helps to break up clods of earth so that sowing, in a couple of months, will be much easier. If you have rough ground on your allotment, get in there with a mattock or fork and break it into clumps, then let the evil February conditions do the hard work for you! Spread well-aged manure or compost on your potato bed and fork it in a bit – again, the weather will do the job of breaking it down into the soil for you, this month.

If you've already started sowing in your greenhouse, stand in it for 15 minutes or so at the end of the day and **check for draughts**. It takes that long for us to notice the faint chill breeze that can wipe out a tray of precious seedlings in no time at all. Ventilation is necessary, but draughts are dangerous. We often find a couple of cracks have developed where our glass panels meet the greenhouse frame and they can easily be filled with putty. Our ventilator is covered with a layer of mesh to break up any really howling gales, so the air gets in but it doesn't sweep through. While you're standing there, check your pots and irrigation trays are clean and aren't harbouring overwintering snails or slugs, or woodlice. The woodlice aren't a massive problem, as they only tend to eat rotting vegetation, but if you have a damaged or diseased plant they will help it on its way when it might otherwise have recovered.

If you have **early-flowering fruit trees** like **apricots**, etc., inspect them now for bud growth and if necessary cover with horticultural fleece or old net curtains supported away from the branches to stop frosts taking out the early flowers.

Force a **rhubarb** crown by covering it with a big old bucket if you didn't start off some champagne rhubarb in November.

Crops to harvest

- **Brassicas** – the early **purple sprouting broccoli**, all the **kales** and **Brussels sprouts** should be in full swing.
- **Chard**
- **Chicory**, nicely bleached under buckets, is delicious now.

- **Celery** and **celeriac,** if grown in raised beds or otherwise sheltered from snow and frost.
- **Jerusalem artichokes**
- **Leeks**
- **Parsnips** – remember to keep parsnips covered with fleece or nestled in straw to stop them freezing in the ground, so you can dig them up when you want them.
- Some gardeners have **salsify** or **scorzonera** – we've never managed to get them to germinate well enough on our clay to justify calling them a crop, but if you can grow them, they are delicious this month.

Recipe of the month:

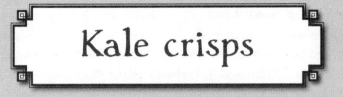

Kale crisps

The first thing to say is that this recipe can be prepared with other crops than kale. Spring greens work well and even winter cabbage can be used, at a pinch, but it's definitely best made with kale and best of all with the red (we like redbor) or black (nero) kale. Between February and April, each kale leaf that you've removed from the plant will sprout a new leaf, and it's this tiny, furled, new growth that makes really good crisps. If you only have large leaves, you need to tear out the large ribs so that you only have the tender growth left. The crisps will end up between a half and a quarter the original size, so bear that in mind as you tear them apart.

The second thing to say is that you don't need to add any salt to these crisps. Ever. They have a salty tang all of their own. I know many recipes suggest salt but I seriously recommend you try making them without salt first: most of us each far too much salt and finding foods we can enjoy without salt should be a priority when we're eating our own crops, as there is 'hidden' salt in so many foods that we buy.

A large bag of kale leaves
Oil
Seasonings

Preheat your oven to 160–180°C/gas mark 3–4, using the lower temperature if your oven runs hot, higher if it runs cool and while it's heating, wash the kale and tear out the ribs if necessary. Dry in a tea towel or in a salad spinner – it needs to be as dry as possible.

In a large plastic bag without air holes put a tablespoon of vegetable oil and your choice of dressings. Pop the kale in, twist the top of the bag (ensuring it is full of air) and hold it firmly as you shake thoroughly to combine the oil, seasonings and kale.

Tip the kale onto two large baking trays and spread it out – don't grease the trays as there will be enough oil on the kale to stop it sticking. Put in the oven for five minutes.

Take the trays out, shake gently to redistribute the kale (it will be shrinking already) and put back in oven for five to seven minutes. You should have dark, crispy, flavoursome crisps.

Kale crisps are crunchy and addictive and even people who despise greens will eat them. Serve them up in front of the TV instead of popcorn, or crush them and sprinkle them on a winter soup instead of croutons. Other great ways to eat them are to strew them on cream cheese that you've spread on a slice of home-baked bread or put them in a big bowl and serve them up with a roast dinner like game chips.

There's no limit to the ingenuity you can bring to the flavourings. Here are just a few of our favourites:

Smoky
½ tsp smoked paprika
1 tsp walnut oil

Oriental

1 tsp soy sauce

1 tsp sesame oil

1 tsp sesame seeds (shake the sauce, oil and kale together, then
add the seeds and shake again before baking)

Spicy

Pinch ground chilli powder

1 tsp mustard seed

½ tsp chilli oil

½ tsp maple syrup

Caesar

1 tsp sunflower oil

½ tsp celery granules (not salt)

½ tsp powdered parmesan (either the stuff you get in tubs at the
supermarket or grate it finely yourself, freeze it in a plastic bag
and then roll over the bag with a rolling pin to really
granulate it).

Use the same method as for the Oriental dressing – adding the
celery granules and parmesan after you've shaken the kale crisps
and oil together.

Epilogue

The great thing about growing your own is that there is never a finish to anything – each year's 'end' is the next season's beginning, each harvest is simply making way for the next crop, each meal is, in part, just a way of fuelling yourself to go out and grow more delicious food.

Knowing how to end a book about an unending pleasure and obsession is difficult: advice sounds preachy and encouragement may be unnecessary. The Chinese say 'All gardeners know better than other gardeners' and I take that as both advice and encouragement. Your way of growing things is an experiment, conducted on the face of the planet itself, whose results you, and you alone, can quantify. When we grow something – flowers, fruit, vegetables or even loofahs, like Celia – we are gardeners and scientists, poets, labourers, cooks, artists and designers. Few hobbies feed all the senses and all the family, save the world and serve the environment, but growing food does all these things and more, so I hope that your obsession flourishes and I would love to hear what results you get from your experiments in growing! Contact me through my website, www.kaysexton.com.

MINDING MY PEAS AND CUCUMBERS

Quirky Tales of Allotment Life

Kay Sexton

£9.99

ISBN: 978-1-84953-135-1

Hardback

When Kay Sexton becomes the proud holder of an allotment, she hopes it will be her first foray towards self-sufficiency for her family. Instead, she finds herself in a strange and hostile world of hosepipe stand-offs and arcane rules and regulations.

She finds her mud-caked wellingtoned feet and successfully navigates her way through allotment-keeping, battling biblical-scale pest invasions, learning the dark arts of the competitive vegetable grower and practising ninja-like disappearing acts to avoid yet another free cucumber from a neighbouring gardener.

Witty, well-observed and with mouth-watering recipes, this book is for anyone who dreams of a slice of the good life.

THE GARDENER'S CALENDAR

Pippa Greenwood

£8.99
ISBN: 978-1-84953-234-1
Hardback

This wonderful and charmingly illustrated reference guide contains specific month-by-month 'to do' lists for ornamental gardens, edible crops and general maintenance, as well as tips on things to look out for, such as pests and how to eliminate them. With diary pages for making your own notes each month, this pocket-sized calendar is a must-have. Whether you're a seasoned gardener or just starting out, this book will become an old and trusted friend.

Have you enjoyed this book?
If so, why not write a review on your favourite website?

If you're interested in finding out more about our books, find
us on Facebook at **Summersdale Publishers** and follow us on
Twitter at **@Summersdale**.

Thanks very much for buying this Summersdale book.
www.summersdale.com